Charles Godfrey Leland

Pidgin-English Sing-Song

Or, Songs and Stories in the China-English Dialect

Charles Godfrey Leland

Pidgin-English Sing-Song
Or, Songs and Stories in the China-English Dialect

ISBN/EAN: 9783744748353

Printed in Europe, USA, Canada, Australia, Japan

Cover: Foto ©Thomas Meinert / pixelio.de

More available books at **www.hansebooks.com**

PIDGIN-ENGLISH SING-SONG

OR

SONGS AND STORIES

IN

THE CHINA-ENGLISH DIALECT.

With a Vocabulary.

BY

CHARLES G. LELAND.

LONDON:
TRÜBNER & CO., LUDGATE HILL.
1876.

[All rights reserved.]

Contents.

	PAGE
INTRODUCTION	1
HINTS TO THE READER	10

BALLADS.

WANG-TI	15
MARY COE	24
SLANG-WHANG	28
PING-WING	29
CAPTAIN BROWN	31
A-LÚM THE BAKER	39
WANG THE SNOB	42
AHONG AND THE MUSQUITO	48
CONFUCIUS AND LA-OU-TSZE	52
THE CAT	56
THE REBEL PIG	59
THE GREEN-TEA LAND	63
MY HEART AND GONG	65
PROVERBS	66
L'OISEAU	68
THE PRINCESS IN TARTARY	69
THE RAT	73
THE PIGEON	74

	PAGE
LITTLE JACK HORNER	75
THE TOYMAN'S SONG	76
CAPTAIN JONES	77
THE BALLAD OF WING-KING-WO	80

STORIES.

CAPTAIN JONES AND THE ARROW	89
CAPTAIN JONES AND HIS MEDICINE-CHEST	90
THE OBEDIENT SERVANT	92
HOWQUA AND THE PEARLS	94
THE COW AND THE COMPRADORE	96
THE CHINESE AND THE JEW	98
THE WOOLLY HEN AND THE RED GOOSE	100
THE TALKING DUCKS	103
THE LITTLE WIFE	107
FIRE AND RIVER	110
NORVAL	112
EXCELSIOR	114

PIDGIN-ENGLISH VOCABULARY	119
PIDGIN-ENGLISH NAMES	137

INTRODUCTION.

PIDGIN-ENGLISH is that dialect of our language which is extensively used in the seaport towns of China as a means of communication between English or Americans and the natives. In its first and lowest form, as given in the vocabularies published for the use of servants, Pidgin is a very rude jargon, in which English words, strangely distorted, owing to the difficulty of representing their sounds in Chinese writing, are set forth according to the principles of Chinese grammar. It is, in fact, word-for-word translation, with very little attempt at inflection or conjugation, as such forms of grammar, as we understand them, do not exist in Chinese. The result of this is naturally that as the vocabulary is very limited, a Chinese learns Pidgin-English with no more difficulty than is presented by acquiring a few hundred words, the pronunciation and grammar of

A

which have been modified to suit those of his own language. In this it corresponds exactly with the *posh an' posh*, or corrupt Rommany dialect spoken by English gipsies, in which Hindi-Persian words follow the English structure.

It is owing to the ease with which Chinese learn this dialect, and the willingness of foreigners to meet them half way in it, that it has spread to such an incredible extent, thereby leading the way towards making English the language of the Pacific. And as Chinese learn a Latin tongue more easily than pure English, it is probable that had it not been for the Pidgin jargon, a corrupt Portuguese would have formed the popular medium of communication between foreigners and natives in China. The number of Portuguese words which now exist in Pidgin-English seem to prove this. As it is, our language in this rude form has spread, and is spreading to such a remarkable extent as to suggest several important problems. The coolie who speaks Pidgin has half his apprehension as to getting on in a foreign country removed, and the anticipated immigration of "millions of the Mongolian race" is beginning to cause serious reflection in America. Therefore Mr Simpson looks forward to a time when it will be necessary to issue the Scriptures in Pidgin, and Captain

Richard Burton gravely remarks in his "Ultima Thule," that "if English, as appears likely, is to become the cosmopolitan language of commerce, it will have to borrow from Chinese as much monosyllable, and as little inflection as possible. The Japanese," he adds, "have already commenced the systematic process of 'pidgeoning,' which for centuries has been used on the West African coast, in Jamaica, and in fact throughout tropical England, Hindostan alone excepted."

The word *pidgin*, if derived, as is generally supposed, from the English word *business*, indicates the difficulty with which Chinese master our pronunciation. It is also characteristic of the jargon, from the incredible variety of meanings which it assumes. As the term *wallah* in Hindu, and that of *engro* in Rommany, are applicable to any kind of active agent, so *pidgin* is with great ingenuity made expressive of every variety of calling, occupation, or affair. As *business* or commerce is the great bond of union between the Chinese and foreign residents, it is not remarkable that this should be the chief and ever-recurring word, and give its name to the language formed in its service.

Pidgin-English, "pure and simple," is found, according to a writer in the "Pall Mall Gazette," only in the native vocabularies published for the benefit of compradores and servants entering the service of English masters. One specimen of this class of work is a little volume of twelve or fifteen pages, and is entitled " A Vocabulary of Words in Use among the Red-Haired People." Its outer cover is adorned with a full-length portrait of one of the red-haired race dressed in the costume of the Georgian period, in breeches and stockings, and armed with stick and sword." [1]

The difficulty which a Chinese experiences in mastering the English pronunciation may be inferred from the fact that in this book brother (elder) is expressed by *pat-lut-ta*, youngest brother

---

[1] Apropos of this vocabulary, my father-in-law, the late Rodney Fisher of Philadelphia, who was for many years resident in China, often related the following. One day calling for his compradore, who did not make his appearance, Mr Fisher overhauled a youth called a *larn-pidyin*, or apprentice, of the class who are admitted by favour of the regular servants to learn what they can of waiting. This tyro, not being able to reply, in great alarm led Mr Fisher to a lower room where a number of his fellow-sub-servants were seated, each with the vocabulary open before him. To one of these he communicated what was wanted, whereupon the superior scholar, turning with incredible dexterity and rapidity from leaf to leaf, read out the following sentence: "He-larn-pidgin-talkee-that-complador-belongey-outside-ko-hom-soon." The terror, real or assumed, of the scholar, coupled with this extraordinary manner of conversation under difficulties, set Mr Fisher into a peal of laughter, which was promptly echoed of course by all the assembled Spelling Bee.

by *yang-shi-lut-ta*, uncle by *yang-ki*, and husband by *ha-sze-man*. The almost insuperable tendency to pronounce *r* as *l* appears in *kī-lin* for green, *lin* for rain, and *lüt* for red—*d* being also a terrible *pièce de résistance* in the native mouth. But no China boy remains faithful to these barbarous words, and he very soon improves *kī-lin* into *kleen* or *gleen*, *lin* to *lain*, and *lüt* to *led*—at which point he long remains stationary. It follows, of course, that there is no settled standard of Pidgin-English, and that anything may correctly claim to be in that dialect, so that it represents English as spoken by a Chinese with some national variation from the English standard. I call special attention to this fact, since among the ballads and prose of this volume there are some which illustrate low-class Pidgin as used by common people, while several of the songs must be understood as coming from a Chinese who, having made much greater progress in English, is desirous of writing it. Unless this allowance be fairly made, those who only know Pidgin-English from its more imperfect utterances will be inclined to think that in several instances I have introduced too many English words and "first-chop" phrases. I may, however, be allowed to plead **per contra** that two distinguished Anglo-

Chinese scholars, Professor R. K. Douglas and H. A. Giles, with other proficients who have paid much attention to Pidgin-English, were so kind as to take great interest in this work while it was in progress, aiding me by correction, criticism, and contribution of material of every kind, and that they consider the language of the songs and stories as generally appropriate and correct.

Pidgin, it may be observed, is now the generally accepted spelling of the word in the Anglo-Chinese newspapers. The dialect is very extensively spoken on the whole sea-board of China, and in the Straits; nor is it unknown in India, while its use is rapidly extending to the interior. It may be true, as Professor Douglas observes, that " of late English masters and mistresses in China are beginning to learn Chinese, and that grammars, dictionaries, and vocabularies in the local dialects are now beginning to find their way into houses into which they have never hitherto been admitted;" while, "on the other hand, a generation of Chinamen is growing up which has learned to speak English grammatically." Yet as real Pidgin-English is, after all, only Chinese, both as to structure and sound, with English words, it is evident that scores of common people will acquire it where one will learn English correctly. It is a curious fact, which has been observed by three of my friends—Messrs Giles, Simson, and Ng-Choy—that instances occasionally occur in which Chinese from different districts, speaking very different dialects, have recourse to "Pidgin" as a medium of conversation, just as men of different nations in the Levant were at one time wont to use the *lingua franca*.

I trust that the critical reader will make allowance for the difficulty of spelling a jargon for which no standard is established, and which varies with every speaker. One gentleman, many years resident in China, thinks that the word *have* should be written as in English; a well-educated native to whom Pidgin was as a boy a step-mother tongue is positive that *hab* is the popular pronunciation, while the printed Chinese vocabulary for servants gives *hop*. The same difficulty is found as to *th*, which is in the mouth of a beginner either the Spanish or English *d*, or a plain *t*, but which is by many given correctly enough. If I have sometimes given one and sometimes the other pronunciation, it is not through carelessness; and I have done so in such a manner as to illustrate different phases of expression. But actual consistency is rendered impossible by the fact that one man often gives different sounds to the same letters. The same difficulty exists as to words which are well known to many persons but not to others. A few will be found in this collection which are possibly not familiar to the oldest European proficients in Pidgin. They are all drawn from the Chinese vocabulary already referred to, and are probably known to most Chinese, who, however, soon drop them.

I have placed at the end of this work the well-known and popular version of "Norval," which first appeared at least forty years ago, and that of "Excelsior"—the names of the authors being unknown to me. I have been informed by an American gentleman who has paid attention to the subject, that a Pidgin-French is developing itself in the Chinese ports, but of this I have obtained no specimens.

It is not pretended that the language of the rhymes and stories in this volume will all be readily and immediately familiar to any person who may take it in hand, but it is certain that with a very little attention they can all be soon mastered. For those who expect to meet with Chinese, either in the East or California, this little book will perhaps be useful, as qualifying them to converse in Pidgin. There are in all not more than thirty altogether foreign or strange words in ordinary use, and a number of these are familiar to all persons of the least general information. What remains can present no difficulty to any one who can understand negro minstrelsy or baby talk.

CHARLES G. LELAND.

HINTS TO THE READER.

CHINESE find great difficulty in pronouncing the letter R, which in their mouths becomes L; therefore the Italic *l* throughout this book indicates *r*. This change is not uncommon in English, and in fact most of the peculiarities in the sounds of Pidgin-English, with many of its other variations, will be recognised by all mothers and nurses. *Th* is often pronounced correctly enough by Chinese whose English is in other respects very imperfect. But with all beginners, and sometimes with those more advanced, it is either *t*, *d*, or the Spanish *d*. *Lo* is frequently added for euphony's sake to words ending with a vowel or liquid. It has no meaning. The same is the case with all the vowels, especially in the *ee* which may at will terminate any word—*e.g.*, *chilo*, a child; *clylo*, to cry. *He, she*, or *it*, may all be expressed, as in Chinese, by *he*, and *they* by the same pronoun.

I, me, my, mine, we, our, ours, are included in *my.*

If Pidgin-English were strictly reduced to its natural principles, there would be in it neither conjugation nor inflection, singular nor plural. Tense as well as different shades of possession and qualification are expressed by the ingenious use of *hab, hab-got, belongey, catchee,* and *can do.* Thus, "*There is* a man within," is given as "Hab got one piecee man room-inside," which is literally translated from the Chinese. *Catchee* indicates possession or ownership—*e.g.,* "He catchee too-muchee dollar,"—He is very rich. *Belongey* is a curious application of the English *belong* to many meanings. Thus, "My belongey China-side," is readily intelligible as meaning "I am a native of China;" but we find a wide deviation from the original sense in "You belongey too-muchee sassy, *galaw*,"—You are indeed too impudent. *Can do* is a simple expression of ability or power, and is often used as the synonym for *yes,* while *no can do* is a favourite negative. By intonation *can do* is a common form of interrogation— *e.g.,* "Can do chow-chow?"—Are you able to eat?

Almost every form of verbal utterance is set forth by *talkee. My talkee he,* may mean I do, did or will tell him, say to him, ask him, inform him; while *that law talkee so-fashion* must be translated " the law expresses itself, or is expressed, thus."

Maskee means all right, in spite of, notwithstanding, but, however, or "anyhow." In the poem " Bamboo" it is used as meaning *without*. " Maskee that ting my no can do." The native vocabulary gives *maskee*, " it is all good." *Galow, galaw, g'low,* or *galā,* has no special meaning, but, like *halt* in South German and *ajā* in Rommany, is much used as an intensitive. The same is the case with *Ch'hoy!* and *Ph'ho!* In many cases it is quite equivalent for *indeed*.

"In Chinese," says Professor R. K. Douglas, "there is always inserted between the numeral and the substantive to which it applies, a word which it is customary to call a classifier, since it points to the kind of object represented by the substantive. For example, instead of saying 'two knives,' a Chinaman would say 'two-to-be-held-in-the-hand-knives,' or instead of table he would say 'one-length-table.' These various classifiers the authors of Pidgin-English have melted down into one word, 'piece.' The writer, therefore" (of the "Vocabulary of Words in Use among the Red-Haired Barbarians"), " translates the Chinese equivalent of our indefinite article as one pe-sze,—

one piece; and a knife he would render by one pe-sze-nai-fo." Consequently "one piece" in pure Pidgin always sets forth *a* or *an*, and in many cases it follows *that*—*e.g.*, "That piecee man no hab catchee d*l*inko,"—That man has nothing to drink.

It should be observed that it is impossible to reduce Pidgin-English, and especially its verbs, to rule. The same man who uses "my talkee he" to intimate that he does, did, or will speak to another, may in the next breath elevate his style enough to say, "my hab talkee" and "my go-talkee." In a letter now before me a gentleman to whom I have been indebted for assistance says, "For four years I have conversed all day long in that language [*i.e.*, Pidgin-English], and have found that it varies a good deal, according to every one's fancy."

He is often substituted for *the* in Pidgin-English. This possibly originated in the dislike to utter *th*, which characterises the first stage of transition from Chinese.

Th, which is often pronounced correctly enough as in English, may be heard at other times as *d*, *t*, or *t'h*, which latter may be regarded as the effort to pronounce correctly, but which results in a rapid succession of *t* by the aspirate.

Pidgin-English Sing-Song.

Wang-ti.

LAST year my look-see plum-t*l*ee all
flower all-same he snow,
T'his sp*l*ing¹ much plenty snowflake
all-same he plum-t*l*ee blow.
He snowflake fallee, meltee, he *l*ed leaf
turnee b*l*own,²
My makee first-chop sing-song how luck go
uppy-down.³

One tim belongey⁴ China-side one student-man
Wang-ti,
He wantchee be one manda*l*in, he wantchee gettee
high.
In Fo*l*est of he Pencils⁵ he hopee name to see,
He wantchee go in Gate of Hung⁶ an' takee first
deg*l*ee.

---

¹ Spring.   ² Brown.
³ These four verses are taken from a Chinese poem.
⁴ There was in China.
⁵ *Hon-lam*, the Forest of Pencils, or the highest degree of literary graduates.
⁶ *Cho-yap-hung-moon* (Canton), entering the Gate of Hung, *i.e.*, obtaining the first degree in the school of Confucius.

Suppose one man no catchee cash, he no can play at game,
Supposey pigeon no hab wing, can no make fly all-same.
Wang-ti he t*l*y fly-up-can-go,[1] he workee hard for some,
But all-same one fire-*l*ocket stick he makee fly-down-come.[2]

But bat by night may blongey, b*l*ight-sun,[3] a butterfly.
One tim you catchee angel s'pose you look-see devil —kwei.[4]
Wang-ti no pass—he no can do—he no can catch deg*l*ee,
You make ear-hear, I talkee how t'his all come good fo' he.

One night Wang-ti go walkee—he feel like loney goose;
How állo study, '*m-chung-yung*[5]—he never hit t'he use.
How some man pass an' catch deg*l*ee while he stick fass' behind,
Like one big-piecee *l*ock[6] while waves fly pass' him on t'he wind.

---

[1] To rise, an ascent.
[2] *Fe-lok-loy*, fly-down-come, a descent or fall.
[3] Bright-sun, *ming-yat*, *i.e.*, to-morrow.   [4] *Kwei*, a devil.
[5] '*M-chung-yung*, not hit the use, *i.e.*, was useless, or in vain.
[6] Rock.

He tinkee deep, he walk like sleep *man-man*[1] inside a wood,
Wat-tim[2] he hea*l*ee bobbe*l*y[3] where olo Joss-house[4] stood.
Wang-ti he tink 'um devilos an' wantchee walkee wide,
He neva tink t'hat Joss-house hab got one-man room-inside.[5]

Just t'hen he savvy la-li-loong[6]-some tief-man muchee bad
Hab wantchee kill one fo*l*eigner, an' catchee állo had.
T'his fan-yun[7] he get knockee-down he look-see colo[8] clay,
But Wang-ti pull he 'volver out an' *l*obber-man *l*un 'way.

Wang-ti he pickee st*l*anger up an' helpee all he can,
He find 'um one young *fa-ke-kwok*[9]—a flower-flag-nation-man.
Wang-ti he take t'hat Me*l*ican—he ve*ll*y good can do,
An' put 'um in he littee bed an' pay 'um some sam-shu.[10]

---

[1] *Man-man*, slowly. [2] *Wat-tim*, when.
[3] *Bobbd*y, noise. [4] *Joss-house*, a temple.
[5] Within, *i.e.*, that anybody was within.
[6] He knew that thieves. [7] *Fan-yun*, a foreign man.
[8] Cold as clay.
[9] *Fa-ke-kwok*, flower-flag-nation, *i.e.*, American.
[10] *Sam-shu*, or *sam-shoo*, rice spirits.

B

He Me*l*ican he soon get well an' walk top-side he
t*l*acks,¹

And muchee-much chin-chin² Wang-ti fo' all he nicee
acts.

T'hey gettee f*l*in,³ so muchee f*l*in t'hey each belongey
half;

T'hat Yankee name he Doolittle; he makee photo-
g*l*af.

If you th*l*ow rice in *l*iver, an' *l*iver wailo⁴ f*l*ee,

You sartin sure some mornin' t'hat rice swim down
to sea.

If f*l*in catch someting inside heart,⁵ he not'her f*l*in
can know,

So Wang-ti talkee Doolittle he tubble an' he woe.

He talk: "It b'longey *my* pidgin to study fo'
deg*l*ee,

My tellee all, galaw,⁶ suppose you give ear-hear⁷ to
me;

My wantchee be one first-class man an' pass examination."

"I see," said Mister Doolittle; "you missed it—like
darnation."

---

¹ *Top-side his tracks*, on his footprints, *i.e.*, upright.
² *Chin-chin*, revere, thank.   ³ *Flin*, friend.
⁴ *Wailo*, goes away, runs.   ⁵ In his mind.
⁶ *Galaw*, a meaningless word.
⁷ *Ne-pee-ee-to-teng*, you give ear-hear, *i.e.*, listen.

"Now," talk Wang-ti, "t'hat Tai-fo-neen[1] he coming *l*ound again,
Suppose my no pull th*l*oo dis tim my life be állo vain,
My be all-same one *lô* flower wat-tim he fadee dead."[2]
"*That* ain't the way," said Doolittle; "I vum to go ahead."

"In olo tim," talk he Wang-ti, "man p*l*intee littee book,
Man hide 'um in he pigtail—or some-side—hookey-c*l*ook.[3]
T'hat book belongey Classics, but Government be pat,
An' talk he killee p*l*inta-man wát makee book like t'hat.[4]

"Suppose my catch dat littee book to hide in *my* pigtail,
My'd walk chop-chop[5] *l*ight th*l*oo *Fo-shee*[6]—for my could neva fail.

---

[1] *Tai-fo-nín* (or *neen*), the great examination year, when the Kuy-yun degrees are conferred.
[2] Like a lily when faded.
[3] *Hookey-clook*, by hook or by crook. Like the Indian Baboos, Chinese sometimes attempt such phrases.
[4] I am informed by a Chinese friend that the penalty extends to the students who attempt to use such hidden helps.
[5] *Chop-chop*, speedily.
[6] *Fo-shee*, examination in the last of the three years.

T'hen my belongey big *tai-pan*[1] an' muchee happy too."

"I vum!"[2] said Mister Doolittle, "I'll fix that thing for you.

"I s'pose when you're examined, if 'tisn't all my eye,
They let you wear your spectacles?"—"T'hey do," say poor Wang-ti.
"Wall, then," say Mister Doolittle, "if you expect to pass,
You've got to get yourself a pair—of magnifyin' glass.

"And secondly, about them books you want for your degree,
I can photograph the Scriptures—complete—inside a pea.
In fact I've seen the London 'Times'—and that's exactly true—
On the leetle end of nothin'—and read it easy too.

"And if the thing will help you—if nothin' else avails,
I'll photograph them Classics upon your finger-nails;
I see you wear 'em awful long (for gougin', I suppose)—
I'd put the Astor Library upon such nails as those."

---

[1] *Tai-pan*, head-man, boss (a slang expression).
[2] *Vum*, vow (Yankee).

I think the stuff is in us—so, by gum, let's put it
 through!
We'll ring into them College dons—and mighty
 han'some, too;
And *you* shall shine as Number One and do the thing
 first-chop,
And be the Grand Panjandrum with a button on
 your top.

T'hey catchee book—t'hey muchee work—t'hey
 keepee awful mum.
T'he books of olo Kung-fou-tsze[1] were all on Wang-ti's
 t'hum.
He blessy goodee Me*l*ican t'hat day t'hey makee
 f*l*ins
When allo larnin t'hat he wantch'[2] was at he finga-
 ins.

On t'he eight' day of he eight' moon g*l*ate bobbe*l*y
 hab been
Fo' G*l*and Examination—wát 'um call he Tai-fo-neen.
T'hey look-see allo student-men insidee he pigtail,
But neva tink of littee spots on Wang-ti's finga-nail.

He look-see muchee innocen', he look-see muchee wise,
Hab catch one piece new spectacle t'hat sit top-side
 he eyes.

---

[1] *Kung-fou-tsze*, Confucius.
[2] *Wantch'* for *wantchee*, want.

T'hey lock 'um up in littee house t*l*ee day till allo done,
An' t'hen Wang-ti come out *Tai-pai*[1]—first-chop an' Numpa One!

Wang-ti hab got t'hat ting *maskee*[2]—Wang-ti he mighty g*l*and,
He go top-side all-not'ha in állo China land.
But allo tim no man can tell or savvy what it meant
How Doolittle catch cont*l*acts f*l*om he China Gove*l*nment.

MORAL-PIDGIN.

My sposey sometim, one tim you hab cuss-um poor Chinee,
It b'longy betta makee f*l*in t'han catch one inimy.
You makee my one iron-face—my tink you betta t*l*y
To do all-same he Doolittle long-side he f*l*in Wang-ti.

S'pose *you* much smart an' *he* much smart—my neva makee joke,
You betta make all-same, you two, to cheatee ot'ha folk.
Chinee an' Yankee in one firm could squeezee whole worl' d*l*y:—
Dis my g*l*ate mo*l*al-pidgin of he sto*l*y of Wang-ti.

---

[1] *Tai-pai*, first; slangily, boss.
[2] *Maskee*, anyhow, despite opposition, all right.

NOTE.—My no savvy dat man Wang-ti, no can talkee supposey dis be pukkha stoly. Wat-tim Massa leed my dis sing-song, my talk he, "No plintee dat befo' you tinkee-leason top-side 'um. S'posey dat sing-song go China-side—more dan tlee handirt millium Chinee get he nailos specklum an' go fo' examination. Allo he China Govelnment wailo devilo top-side-bottom-side. No man makee good-pidgin outside allo dat bobbely, 'cept he one photoglaph-man or one look-see-speckle-man." But Massa makee velly much bad-heart—talk he plintee allo-same. My no tinkee he so bad-heart-man.

AH CHUNG.

P.S.—Any gentleum dat look-see dis, who savvy how to make photoglaphs, an' wantchee give lesson cheapee, may catchee one scholar, s'posey he lite to my 'dress. Also s'posey any man wantchee sell or consign magnifyum look-see speckles, he can hearee of one piecee gentleum who go China-side, fo' long.

Mary Coe.

N he city of Whampo'
    Lib Joss-pidgin-man [1] name Coe.
    Massa Coe, he missiona*l*y,
    Catchee one cow-chilo [2] Ma*l*y.

Fáta-man [3] he *l*eadee book,
Ma*l*y talkee wit'h he cook;
Good olo fáta talkee Josh,
China-cook he talkee bosh.

All-day he Ma*l*y stand and talk,
Or go outside wit'h cook to walk;
She wantchee much to helpee him,
An' talkee Pidgin allo-tim.

By'mby t'hat Ma*l*y gettee so,
He only talkee Pidgin—*g'low*.[4]
An' fáta so*ll*y to look-see,
She tinkee-*l*eason like Chinee.

---

[1] *Joss-pidgin-man*, clergyman.
[2] *Cow-chilo*, girl (obsolete).
[3] Father.
[4] *G'low, galaw*, a meaningless interjection.

One piecee f*l*in¹ f*l*om Boston come
One day to findee Coe at home,
He sháman² wailo³ open door,
But Ma*l*y *l*un chop-chop before.

T'hat gentleum talkee when he come,
"Is Mister Coe, my dear, at home?"
An' Ma*l*y talk he, ve*ll*y t*l*ue,
"My tinkee dis tim no can do.

"He olo fáta—still as mouse,
He chin-chin Joss top-sidee house.
Allo-tim he make Joss-pidgin,
What you fan-kwei cally 'ligion."

T'hat gentleum much stare *galow*
To hea*l*ee girley talkee so,
He say, "Dear child, may I inquire
Which form of faith you most admire?"

An' Ma*l*y answer he *l*equest,
"My like Chinee Joss-pidgin best;
My love Kwan-Yin⁴ wit'h chilo⁵ neat,
An' Joss-stick smellum muchee sweet.

"Afong our olo cook, down-stair,
He teachee Ma*l*y Chinee p*l*ayer,

---

¹ Friend.   ² *Shámán*, servant (unusual).   ³ *Wailo*, went.
⁴ *Kwan-Yin*, the Chinese goddess of Mercy, represented as holding an infant.   ⁵ *Chilo*, child.

Talk if my chin-chin Fo, ch'hoy![1]
Nex' tim my born, my bornee boy.

An' t'hen my catchee, nicey new,
A 'ittle dacket—towsers, too,
An' *l*un about wit'h allo boys
In bu'ful boots 'at makee noise."

Tear come in he gentleum eyes,
An' t'hen he anger 'gin to *l*ise ;
He wailo[2] scoldee Massa Coe
For 'glectin' littee Ma*l*y so.

An' Massa Coe feel ve*ll*y sore,
An' go an' scold he comp*l*adore ;
An' comp*l*adore all ho*ll*or[3] shook,
*L*un downy stairs an' bang 'he cook.

An' worsey allo-allo pain,
Ma*l*y go Boston homo 'gain ;
No fi*l*ee *cl*acker[4] any more,
Nor talk wit' cook an' comp*l*adore.

MORAL-PIDGIN.

If Boston girley be let go,
She sartin sure to b'lieve in Fo ;[5]
An' he nex' piecee in he plan,
Is to *l*un *l*ound an' act like man.

---

[1] "Tells me if I pray to Budda-ha, ha !"   [2] *Wailo*, went.
[3] *Hollor*, horror.   [4] Fire crackers.   [5] *Fo*, Buddha.

So, littee chilos, mindee look,
An' neva talkee wit' t'he cook ;
Fo' if you do, firs' ting you know,
You catchee fits—like Ma*l*y Coe.

NOTE.—Dis one muchee pukkha[1] sto*l*y my tell Massa 'bout he littee Ma*l*y—all-same my no hab tinkee he can do one piecee sing-song 'bout 'um. But one ting no be pukkha. Wat-tim Massa talkee my to makee one piecee Mo*l*al-Pidgin, my say—

"Suppose you bad, you hab to go
To Boston, all-same Ma*l*y Coe."

Massa he talkee, "Boston-man no likee dat pidgin : Bos'on-man too muchee good to my." So Massa makee he sing-song as belongey, an' my makee dis note as belongey.

AH CHUNG.

---

[1] *Pukkha*, true.

Slang-Whang.

SLANG-WHANG, he Chinaman
   Catchee school in Yangtsze-Kiang,
   He larn-pidgin sit top-side g*l*oun',
An' *l*eedee lesson upside down,
Wit'h *Yatsh-ery—patsh-ery, snap* an' *sneeze*,
So fash' he chilo *l*eed Chinese.

Slang-Whang, when makee noise,
Wit'h he pigtail floggee állo boys,
Allo this pidgin much tim go,
What tim good olo Empe*l*or Slo.
An' no more now in Yangtsze-Kiang
Hab got one teacher good like Slang.

Ping-Wing.

PING-WING he pie-man son,
    He ve*ll*y worst chilo állo Can-tón,
    He steal he mother picklum mice,
An th*l*owee cat in bilin' rice.
Hab chow-chow[1] up, an' "Now," talk he,
"My wonda' where he meeow cat be?"

Ping-Wing he look-see, tinkey fun
Two piecee man who shleep in sun,
Shleepee sound he yeung-ki,[2] fáta,[3]
Ping tie 'um pigtail allo togata,
T'hen fi*l*ce c*l*acker an' offy *l*un,
T'hat piecee ve*ll*y bad pie-man son.

Ping-Wing see gentleum wailo—go
He scleamee, "*Hai yah—fan-kwei lo!*"
All-same you savvy in Chinee,
"One fo*l*eign devil lookee see!"

---

    [1] Ate.   [2] Uncle (unusual, C.V.)
    [3] *Fáta*, father (C.V.)

But gentleum t'hat pidgin know,
He catchee Ping and floggum so,
T'hat állo-way f*l*om that day, maskee
He ve*ll*y good littee Chinee.

NOTE.—Dis no pukkha sto*l*y. No hab got one so-bad piecee boy állo China-side wat makee so to he fatha.

AH CHUNG.

Captain Brown.

SOMETIM you look-see piecee wave he walkee mountain-high,
Jist t'hen wind knock foam top-side off an' blow 'um up to sky.
Jist so my heart walk up inside—befo' he sinkee down
My makee foamy sing-song up 'bout olo Captin B*l*own.

He b'long one piecee Fa-ke,[1] one flower-flagee-man,
We callo so on China-side—you callo Me*l*ican.
Chinee make han'some talkee—my neva tellee lie—
He betta sing-song catch inside t'han allo you Fan-kwei.[2]

He Captin B*l*own he too[3] much nice—so good inside he can,
T'his talkee t'hat of állo men he first-chop good-heart man,

---

[1] *i.e.*, He was an American.
[2] He has more poetry in his soul than all you foreign devils.
[3] *Too* signifies *very* in Pidgin-English.

. He piggies wailo¹ afta he—t'hat horse long-side he sheep,
It alway makee Captin cly to hear one chilo weep.

One day he walk outside Ow-moon—t'his talkee² town Macâo—
Inside one piecee plison he healee awful low.³
Some piecee man t'hey scleamee bad, an' too much cly to he,
T'hat olo Captin ask chop-chop, "Wat pidgin⁴ t'his can be?"

An' one mafoo⁵ he talkee him, while Captin hold he bleath.
He all be Tai-ping lebel man who soon muss catchee deat'h,
An' t'hat he leason of wát-for he makee such a low,
Befo' he gettee head cut off he catchee no chow-chow.

T'hat plisoner be most starvee, an' so he scleamee 'way;
But s'pose he thlow 'um penny, t'hat feed 'um fo' a day.
Me solly say t'hat Captin Blown talk someting velly bad,
But cly like littee baby—an' pay 'em⁶ állo had.

---

¹ *Wailo*, go, follow.   ² This means.
³ *Low*, a row, riot.   ⁴ What affair.
⁵ *Mafoo*, horse-boy.   ⁶ Gave them.

Chop-dolla', flanc, an' sapek,[1] an' cash of állo sort,
All-same one piecee sailee-man[2] he catch in evely port,
He makee one good sailee jerk so nicee as he can,
It állo got thloo winda' to he starvin' plisona'-man.

When Captin Blown next Sunday he wailo[3] to Joss-house,
He make all-same as állo-tim,[4] he sittee still as mouse;
But when he healee talkee 'bout captive an' plisoner sad,
He holler out lesponse so loud he people tink he mad.

Now s'posey you make good pidgin to man t'hat b'lieve in Fo,[5]
Sometim you sartin catch 'um back—s'pose *he* be dead *galow*.
When állo seem be wailo 'way[6] he sure to catch he wish,
When you make find one pond dly up you sure look-see t'he fish.[7]

But Captin wailo on all light[8]—jis' likee t'his sing-song,
He sail to San Flancisco, an' forget he *la-li-loong*;[9]

---

[1] *Sapek*, the French word for the common China coin.
[2] *Sailee*, sailor (*seli*, C.V.)   [3] *Wailo*, went.
[4] Did as usual.
[5] Suppose you do a kindness to a believer in Buddha.
[6] Gone.   [7] Chinese proverb.   [8] Went on all right.
[9] *La-li-loong*, the thieves.

C

But when he come to Golo Land[1] he so*ll*y an' hab care,
He wantchee catch one chit[2] f*l*om hom, but findee no chit t'here.

He wantchee hear how máta[3] an' he one piece wifey be,
He wantchee larn how fáta[4] an' chilo all look-see.
He catchee plenty tubble inside an' outside too,
Man makee longey facey when no savvy wát can do.

One day he walkee top-side bund,[5] t'here he look-see one f*l*in,
Who talk, "*Hai yah,* my olo boy!" and askee how he been;
T'hen Captin B*l*own tell inside-out wát blongey állo, t*l*ue,
An' ask he f*l*in to talk *maskee*[6] wát devilo he can do.

T'hat f*l*in he tink one piecee tim, t'hen talkee Captin B*l*own,
"Hab-got one spi*l*it-mejum here—he best in állo town;
Supposey you look-see t'hat man—supposey go tonight,
He talkee you how wifey be—t'hat pidgin all come *l*ight."

---

[1] *Golo land,* gold land, the land of gold.
[2] *Chit,* a letter.   [3] *Máta,* mother (C.V.)   [4] Father.
[5] *Bund,* embankment, quay.   [6] *Maskee,* right.

Suppose in t'his worl' man no catch someting he wantchee know,
He go to spi*l*it-meejeum and get he savvy [1] so.
Wát-tim Chu-mái-chin no hab cash to buy one lamp fo' night,
He makee hole th*l*oo wall maskee, an' steal he neighbour light.[2]

(Now when my talkee mejum an' spi*l*it-*l*appin'—*hai!*
My savvy t'at you tinkee he found out by you *fan-kwei!*
My f*l*in, you b*l*utal igno*l*ance make fall one piecee tear,
Chinee hab catch t'at pidgin now t'his tenty taushan year.

Supposey one man China-side, he wantchee savvy how
He f*l*in or chil' or fáta [3] be—when die-lo long, *galow.*
He makee pen of peach-t*l*ee wood—no ot'her sort muss get—
T'hat spi*l*it come an' *l*ap an' *l*ap and *l*ite like one *planchette.*)

---

[1] *He savvy,* his information.
[2] It is said of Chu-mái-chin, a famous scholar, that when he had no money with which to buy candles, he bored a hole through the wall and read by a ray of light thus obtained.
[3] Friend, child, or father.

He Captin go to mejum—an' mejum go to sleep,
An' sleep go into wind-fire land, where állo ting be deep.
T'hat mejum jist hab catchee light—jist go to talkee t*l*ue,
When állo-once he stop an' say, "T'his pidgin no can do.

"My catch one spi*l*it tell my all—but he can no be heard;
Some nother spi*l*it hab got hea*h*'—he no can talkee word.
T'hey makee muchee bobbe*l*y—too muchee c*l*owd a*l*oun'—
T'hey wantchee muchee bad one tim to chin-chin Captin B*l*own.

"T'hey talk all-same t'hey savvy[1] you—t'hey all can do, maskee.[2]
Such facie man[3] in állo-tim my neva hab look-see.
My tinkee muchee cu*l*io—he állo be China-man;
But állo hab he head cut off, and holdee in he han'.

"One piecee man hold up he head to my by he pig-tail,
It talk, 'My blongey p*l*ison once—my lib in China jail.

---

[1] *Savvy*, know.
[2] They are determined to do so, anyhow.
[3] Such looking men.

We catchee plenty hunga' t'here—we scleamee up
 an' down,
But only one man helpee us—an' t'hat was Captin
 Blown.

"'T'hat Captin he make plenty good fo' állo my
 galaw,
Until we catchee head cut off, as belongey China law.
An' eva' since we spilits all go walkee uppy down,
We wantchee to look-see one tim to chin-chin[1] Cap-
 tin Blown.

"'If Chinee no can make chin-chin he catch no good
 inside,
Supposey he be állo live—supposey he hab died.
So here we chin-chin plenty nice—but fo' we say
 "good-night,"
My wantchee talkee Captin Blown—he family all
 light.'"

MORAL-PIDGIN.

My flin, supposey you hab leed he book of Kung-
 fou-tsze,
You larn t'hat állo gleatest man he most polite man
 be,
An' on polite-pidgin Chinee beat állo, up or down—
T'his is he molal-pidgin of he song of Captin Blown.

---

[1] *Chin-chin.* In this relation, to manifest gratitude and politeness, to show good manners.

NOTE.—Dis one of Massa he own sto*l*y. My no savvy¹ s'posey belongy pukkha² or no—s'posey no, my tink he tol-oli³ good look-see-pidgin sto*l*y.⁴ It catchee some piecee muchee good talkee 'bout spi*l*it-*l*appin' China-side; long-side one ve*ll*y good mo*l*al-pidgin. Dis good-party *á*llo *my* talkee.

AH CHUNG.

---

¹ *Savvy*, know.   ² Is true or not.   ³ *Tol-oli*, tolerably (C. V.)
⁴ Apparently true, will pass for truth.

A-lúm the Baker.

BOUT he tim when olo debilo
    Sp*l*ead he claws top-sidee land,
All-sam time he fan-kwei *l*ebel
    Makee bobbe*l*y allo hand;
When he Emp*el*or tellum wailo,
    But he English keepee come,
Jist t'at tim in town of Hong-Kong
    Lib one baka'-man, A-lúm.

Manda*l*in make p*l*oclamation:
    "S'posey kill one piece *fan-kwei*,
Chinaman catch hantun[1] dolla',
    And he *l*isee ve*ll*y high.
S'pose he killee sixy-seven,
    T'hen he catchee plenty tin;
Top-side t'at, he Son of Heaven
    Make t'at man a manda*l*in."

Olo A-lúm tinkee one tim
    Allo t'his pidgin in he head:

---

[1] *Hantun*, one hundred (C.V.)

"In Hong-Kong two tousand *fan-kwei*
    Buy flom Chinaman he blead.
S'pose my pizen only halfee,
    T'at can makee plitty sum;
An' my catchee colal button!"
    Talkee baka'-man, A-lúm.

So A-lúm he catchee pizen,
    Plenty pizen állo town;
Inside bleakfast-lolls he make it,
    And t'at lolls he bakum blown.
But as hunter lib by killin'
    He one tim at last get kill,
So by'mby t'his Chinee baka'
    He get done more blowner still.

For good pizen man pay dolla',
    An' no tief-man flin be tlue,
An' A-lúm he catchee scholar
    Who much wantchee dolla' too;
So while all he dough was lisin,
    T'his come in larn-pidgin's head,
He make steal most állo pizen,
    An' put *plaster* in instead.

An' he sellee állo pizen,
    'Fo' he lolls make turnee blown;
An' he catchee állo dolla',
    An' he wailo outee town.

Wailo, wailo to t'he fan-kwei,
    An' before t'he *l*isee sun
He hab talkee állo sto*l*y
    What he baka' wantchee done.

But befo' he makee stop he,
    Muchee man chow-chow t'at b*l*ead,
An' too plentee catchee sickee,
    But my tinkee no catch dead.
Ai ! it makee muchee bobbe*l*y,
    Fo' he talkee eve*l*y tongue ;
An' larn-pidgin catchee dolla',
    But he baka'-man get hung.

MORAL-PIDGIN.

Man hab talkee, t'his not first tim
    T'at A-lúm make bobbe*l*y so ;
An' t'at since he deadee wailo,
    Still he makee kill, *galow*.
It was alway olo custom
    An' to-day my hea*l*ee said
V*ell*y often how he Alum
    Makee pizen baka's b*l*ead.

NOTE.—My tinkee inside dis sing-song Massa no hab catchee p*l*opa bunder. T'at one piecee man A-lúm he no catchee hang—he wailo way, my tinkee can be he stop China-side inside, t'his tim, now.[1] My chin-chin Massa too-muchee he please ixcuse t'his talkee.   AH CHUNG.

---

[1] A-lúm was really arrested, tried, and acquitted, though his guilt is still generally believed in.

Wang the Snob.

CHINA-SIDE one tim belongey
    Man name Wang, he too much likee
    F*l*in who catchee plenty dolla',
F*l*in who catchee first-chop button,
Manda*l*in an' all-same people,
Poor-man f*l*in t'hat Wang no wantchee.

One tim Wang he makee t*l*avel,
Makee stop one night in Joss-house.
He go sleep, by'mby he wakee
Iniside all-samee Joss-house;
Wang he tink he hea*l*ee talkee,
Go outside, what for?—he wantchee
To look-see wat makee bobbe*l*y.
Wat you tink he Wang he findee?
He look-see two piecee coffin,
Two piece dead man inside coffin,
One to not'ha' makee talkee.

Wang look-see at he two coffin;
Makee *l*eed he chop¹ top-side-um.
One chop talkee how he dead man
He wat lib insidee coffin,
He one manda*l*in,—he not'ha'
Coffin blongy one poor schola',
Wat hab nebba catchee dolla',
Wat hab nebba catchee button.
T'hat sort man he Wang no likee;
Allo t'hat sort he send devilo.

Wang he go to first-chop coffin,
To he mand'*l*in an' chin-chin 'um,
Burnee joss-stick, talkee p*l*itty,
Knock he head all-same one hamma';
Make kow-tow in China fashion,
T'hen by'mby he chin-chin someting.
Chin-chin manda*l*in to like he;
Come sometim when he catch sleepee,
Come sometim in d*l*eam look-see 'um.

Wang look-see he poo' dead student,
Turnee nose top-side at dead man;
Talkee to 'um too much saucy,
Talkee t'hat no p*l*opa pidgin,
Stop long-side t'hat not'ha' coffin.
" Wat you wantchee side he mand'*l*in?"

---

¹ Inscription.

Askee Wang. "If you look-see 'um
Inside hell, you lose you facee,
He so big an' you so shmallo."
T'hen he wipee first-chop coffin,
Leavee schola' coffin dusty.

Tlee day wailo in he nightee,
Wang look-see one ghost in shleepee;
Olo man all dlessee han'some,
Muchee first-chop olo person
Wat look-see one pukkha gentlum.
"Hai!" t'at Massa Wang he tinkee,
"T'his he mandalin wat I chin-chin
In he Joss-house, inside coffin;"
So he make chin-chin an' kow-tow.
But he ghost talk, "What for chin-chin!
You no savvy you big foolo,
T'ot'ha' day you talk bad pidgin
Talkey my, *galaw*, too sassy,
Wat-tim you look-see my coffin."
"*Hai yah!*" talkee Wang, "my tinkee
You must blongey t'ot'ha' dead man.

"My tink you belongy mand'lin."
"No," talk ghost, "my blongey schola'.
You belongey one big foolo.
My jus' now look-see dat mand'lin
Down in hell he one poor begga',
Bottom-side in hell he stop now,

No hab got one cash to bless 'um ;
But my be, now my hab die-lo,
Allo-tim one top-side swell-o
Heaven-pidgin-man—first-choppee,
Tai-pan, tai-pai, numpa one-lo.
But no fea*h!* my talk you someting
S'posey you chin-chin[1] my han'some ;
Burnee my some piece joss-papa',[2]
My no catch bad-heart to you-lo.
No blong *l*eason to make bobbe*l*y,
Betta makee állo p*l*opa.

"Now my tink you wantchee dolla'—
Allo man he wantchee someting;
S'pose you wailo to one go-down[3]
Tu-lip [4] *li* outside dis city,
You look-see one weepee willow.
S'posey t'here you diggee hole-o,
Ch'hoy! you look-see wat you catchee,
Sartin t'here you catchee someting."

Ghost he wailo, Mr Wang he
Too much happy inisidee,
Tinkee nighty go too *man-man*,[5]
Wantchee *bl*ight-sun[6] come *chop-chop*—he

---

[1] Worship me well.
[2] *Joss-paper*, counterfeit bank-bills, or clothing, &c., burned for the dead.   [3] Warehouse, house, &c.
[4] *Tu-lip*, twelve (C. V.)   [5] *Man-man*, slowly.
[6] *Bright-sun*, morning to come quickly.

Wishee hours all glease wit'h cow-oil,
So to makee slip more easy.

Mornin' come an' Wang he wailo [1]
To t'hat go-down—look-see willow;
Mr Wang he makee diggee,
Too much diggee, he no likee
Diggee-pidgin, then he healee
How one man make noise in go-down.
Coolie man come out an' talkee
Mr Wang one tim, an' askee
Wat he devilo ting he wantchee?
What fo' he come t'here an' diggee?
Coolie makee too much bobbely,
Catch one piecee stick an' floggee
Mr Wang, till Wang half die-lo;
Nebba catchee one such floggum
Allo he life—he nebba tinkee
Any man hab catch such floggum.
Wang go homee, Wang go beddy,
An' in beddy too much weepee,
'Cos he be such too-much foolo.
By'mby-lo when he get betta,
Wang he catch more sense inside he,
More-by'mby he often tinkee
Wat he schola' ghost make teach-um.
Allo-time he lib more plopa,
Nebba more kow-tow big people.

---

[1] *Wailo*, hastened.

MORAL-PIDGIN.

S'posey you go make all-samee,
Den you blong five dolla' betta.
Sing-song finish. How you likee?[1]

NOTE.—My catchee muchee so*ll*y inside to talkee[2] hab got snob-man China-side, állo-same Englishee-side, or Me*l*ican. It állo pukkha. But my no belongey hearee dat inside England one piecee ghost-man come f*l*om he deadee to makee he snob *l*epent. Man makee állo-same ting too-muchee betta China-side. My tinkee dat be muchee p*l*opa pidgin fo' ghost to makee. Can-be, Englishee ghosto tinkee he catchee he hand too-muchee fullo, belongey too-much to do, supposey he t*l*y to make állo snobs inside England an' Me*l*ica *l*epent. *Hai*, wat you tinkee?　　　　　　　　　　　　　　AH CHUNG.

---

[1] From a story given in the "Celestial Empire," October 23, 1875.

[2] I regret to admit.

Ahong and the Musquito.

SUPPOSEY you make listen, my sing one piecee song,
My make he first-chop fashion about t'he g*l*ate¹ Ahong;
He b*l*avest man in China-side, or any side about;
My bettee you five dolla', *hai!* he b*l*avest party out.

He only fightee 'skeeta', you tinkee t'hat not much.
No hab one Manchū Tartar t'hat káli² fightee such.
My *l*ather fightee d*l*agon t'hat killee állo³ dead;
T'hat 'skeeta' Ahong killee top-side he Empe*l*or's head.

Ahong he pukkha⁴ baba⁵ no betta can look-see,
Ahong he first-chop swordman—no swordman hood⁶ like he;

---

¹ *Glate*, great. The italic *l* throughout indicates *r*.
² *Káli*, want, dare, care (C.V.)   ³ *Allo*, all.
⁴ *Pukkha*, real or genuine.
⁵ *Baba* (*papa*, C.V.), barber.   ⁶ *Hood*, good (C.V.)

He cuttee men like hair down; he tinkee állo fun:
Hab sword or hab got *l*azor—Ahong he Numpa One.

Man-man[1] one peach-t*l*ee floweree become one piecee peach,
Man-man one littee chilo[2] get wisa' állo men teach;
You catch one piecee *can do;* some day it make you g*l*ate;
Ahong hab larn t'his lesson—to fightee, shave and wait.

My s'pose you tinkee tim much long to stop till bad luck past,
But one big piecee mountain he wind blow down at last;
"An' when by'mby you luck come," I *l*eed in olo song,
"You catch *flee*[3] as 'skeeta'"—for luck not waitee long.

Ahong he Emp*el*o's baba'; one day t'hat come about
To shave he Chilo Heaven he takee *l*azor out,
But jist as he come pidgin top-side he holy head,
He make look-see one piecee ting t'hat állomost make he dead.

There come one *kwei*, one devil—no worsee devil be;
All-same one piecee 'skeeta' t'his devil he look-see.

---

[1] *Man-man*, slowly.   [2] *Chilo*, child.   [3] *Fitee!* quick!

Ahong no see before-tim one pidgin bad like it,
*L*ight on he Empe*l*o's head-side he 'skeeta' makee sit.

Jist t'hen Ahong he catch he chance—one tim of állo tim
One big Joss-pidgin-pidgin[1] chance for állo likee him.
What ting you tink he makee—what ting you tinkee do?
He *go* for t'hat muskito—and cuttee *l*ight in two!

Can-be you s'pose he *cham-tow*[2]—cut off he 'skeeta's head;
Ahong he savvy[3] better t'han makee *chop-chop*[4] dead,
He *l*azor flash like d*l*agon-fire *l*ight t'h*l*oo t'hat 'skeeta' gay,
An' leave he legees standin' up while body fly away.

An' t'hen t'hat Chilo Heaven who savvy all t'hat pass
Top-sidee eart'h, hab look-see t'his (in one big lookee-glass);
He talk t'hat pidgin *how-tak-tsei* (t'hat meanee "ve*ll*y hood"),[5]
An' make Ahong a manda*l*in—which noble all he blood.

---

[1] Divine.   [2] Cut off head.   [3] *Savvy*, know.
[4] Quickly.   [5] *H*ood, good.

T'hat meaney blood before-tim as well as blood to come.
Man make t'his pidgin so-fashion in China land at home,
Suppose you catchee title—it no be p*l*opa g'*l*ow,¹
To be g*l*eater t'han you fáta or g*l*anfáta—and so

T'hey makee állo noble, so-fashion t'hey make do;
T'hey pay² you one hood pedig*l*ee long-side a title too,
You tink *you* catchee *l*eason—my tinkee you look-see
All-same one piecee foolo-man, long-sidey one Chinee.

An' as he Empe*l*o' tinkee Ahong be such a b*l*ick,
He makee pay t'hat barber his own fine walkee-stick;
So it blongey olo cutsom³—which neva *wailo*⁴ way—
Allo baba' hab got stickee in China-side to-day.

Suppose you makee walkee in Canton or Whampo',
You állo-tim see baba'-man who catchee cane, *galow*,
My f*l*in,⁵ when good tim come to do, don't makee stoppee long:
T'his my g*l*ate moral-pidgin of t'he sto*l*y of Ahong.

---

¹ *Galow* or *galaw*, a meaningless word, but much used.
² *Pay*, give.   ³ *Cutsom*, custom.
⁴ *Wailo*, go.   ⁵ *Flin*, friend.

Confucius and La-ou-tsze.

ONE tim he Mr Kung-fou-tsze[1]
   Go talkee olo La-ou-tsze,[2]
      An' all too-muchee chin-chin[3] him
To tell someting 'bout olo tim.
Till, ve*ll*y ang*l*y, La-ou-tsze
Kick up one piecee bobbe*l*y,
An' scoldee bad, he Kung-fou-tsze,
An' talk t'his pidgin, in Chinee.

"He wise man t'at you talkee so,
He deadee wailo[4] longo go.
He bone all *l*otten in he g*l*ave,
Only some piecee word you have,
One piecee word in ole Chinee
You talkee-talkee 'um to me.
He wise man talk to devilo flew,
My wish he talk go dev'lo too.

---

[1] Confucius.
[2] *La-ou-tsze*, a sage founder of the Taou sect.
[3] Implored.   [4] Gone.

CONFUCIUS AND LA-OU-TSZE.

"My s'pose you savv'[1] how má-chin[2] man
Hide up he dolla' állo can,
Make hidee or he manda*l*in
Come squeezee 'way wat má-chin win.
You all-same manda*l*in, I say,
You wantchee[3] squeeze my wisdom 'way.
My savvy someting dat be t*l*ue,
But make no pidgin long-side *you*.

"My lookee you, my so*ll*y see
Wat-piece one foolo-man you be,
You wantchee *l*ise all-same he smoke
Top-sidee headee[4] állo folk.
S'posey you *l*ise one tim—my say,
All-same he smoke you blow away."

When La-ou-tsze have talkee so,
He get top-side one buffalo,
An' *l*idee 'way ac*l*oss he plain,
An' homo[5] nevva com again.
While Kung-fou-tsze, who standee t'here,
All-same one piecee foolo stare,
An' talk, "He wise man La-ou-tsze,
He muchee-much too much for me.

---

[1] *Savvy*, know.
[2] *Má-chin*, merchant (native vocabulary).
[3] *Wantchee*, want.
[4] Above the heads of all.
[5] Home. This retort of La-ou-tsze is historical, nor is it denied by the disciples of Confucius.

"My savvy¹ how he fishee swim,
My savvy bird, top-sidee lim',
My savvy how one deer *l*un by,
My savvy how he d*l*agon fly.
Man catchee fish wit' linee-hook,
T'at bird insidee net get took,
Wit' a*ll*ow deer get shootee so,
But how catch d*l*agon no man know.

"He olo sage, he La-ou-tsze
All-same one d*l*agon look to me;
He talkee állo my facie 'way,²
My catchee no one word to say;
He shuttee-up poo' Kung-fou-tsze,
An' makee my all f*l*aid of he."

MORAL-PIDGIN.

Dis pukkha³ sing-song makee show
How smart man make mistake, galow.
Dere's wisee men no hab p*l*etence,
Who long-side wisdom catchee sense.
Oh! tink, my f*l*in!⁴ oh! tink, ye yout'h,
You wantchee d*l*ain t'hat well of t*l*ut'h.

---

¹ *Savvy*, know.
² *To take one's face away*, the common Chinese 'expression for causing shame or defeat.
³ *Pukkha*, true.   ⁴ *Flin*, friend.

Look-see you bucket, 'fore you t*l*y,
Got *l*opee 'nuf to pump 'um d*l*y.
One piecee mouse can d*l*ink at *l*iver,
But let he mousey t*l*y for ever,
All he can do top-sidee shore
Is squinch[1] he t'hirst an' nuffin more.

[1] Quench.

The Cat.

SUPPOSEY moon make shine t'h*l*oo peach-
blossom.
T'at light long-side he blossom, állo two
Look-see more nicey one for not'her—*hai?*
Suppose my catch one sto*l*y wat belong
He olo tim and make one piecee sing;
You look-see sing-song an' he sto*l*y make
One-not'her muchee betta, nevva fear!
One tim lib China-side one piecee cat,
One day he massa take Joss-pidgin beads
He put bead *l*ound cat neck. He cat look-see
All-same one patele,[1] one Joss-pidgin-man.
Wat-tim he mousey walk outside he hole,
Look-see dat pidgin—see dat cat hab catch
One piecee bead, he mousey too much glad.
An' állo mouse catch too much hood[2] inside,
An' talkee not'her állo so-fashion:
"T'hat piecee cat he blongey ve*ll*y hood,
He make Josh-pidgin állo p*l*opa now.

---

[1] *Padre*, priest.   [2] *Hood*, good (C.V.)

One tim he ve*ll*y bad—but now he 'pent[1]
An' nevva chow-chow[2] mousey any more,
An' állo mousey lib all p*l*opa now;
He go outside what-tim he wantchee go,
An' nevva blongey f*l*aid—he cat no fear.
An' mousey go to sing-song[3] állo tim,
An' takee waifo, chilos walk outside,
An' állo day for állo mousey now,
He be one Feast ob Lantern, *hai! ch'hoy!*"
T'at mousey tink t'at pidgin ve*ll*y nice,
He catchee too much happy iniside,
He makee dancee, galantee, maskee.[4]
· He cat look-see t'at dance, he walk man-man,
No makee bobbe*l*y till wat-tim he come
Long-side he dancee—t'en he *l*un chop-chop[5]
Insidee dance and catch one piecee mouse,
An' makee chow-chow all same olo tim.
He mousey f*l*in all wailo in he hole,
An' állo c*l*y c*l*y—some for he dead f*l*in,
·An' some what-fo'[6] he f*l*aid cat catchee he;
An' állo-tim t'ey make one sing-song,
Sing-song how mousey so*ll*y iniside.
T'at sound all-same he wind top-side t'at pines;
T'at sound all-same one piecee ocean-shell,
" How fashion állo happy ting he come!
How fashion állo happy wailo 'way!

---

[1] Repent.   [2] Eat.   [3] Theatrical entertainments.
[4] Grand and all right.   [5] Rapidly.   [6] Because.

All-same he sunshine top-side mountain-hat.
My tinkee cat hab got be plopa cat,
My tinkee állo sin belongey dead,
My tinkee mousey makee lob and steal
Allo he wantchee, dat one tim hab got
What-tim he saint catch all ting ebbermore.
My tink he cat he makee chin-chin Fo,
My tinkee Puss-cat be Joss-pidgin-man
Who no can chow-chow meat—*hai yah! ph'hoy!*
Dat cat hab cheatee, cheatee, cheatee my;
My tink he hood—he be too bad, *maskee*.
He Joss-pidgin be all look-see pidgin.[1]
My wish t'at cat be dam wit' evelyting,
For állo world be bad, an' all be bad,
An' evely side hab pizen, cats and tlaps:
My no can do make tlust one man no more."

---

[1] *Look-see pidgin*, hypocrisy (Anglo-Chinese newspaper).

The Rebel Pig.

ALLO-SAME one typhoon
   Cut littee flower down,
   Tai-ping 'bellion
Bot'her állo land;
All-same lightning
Knock olo tower down,
Empe*l*o' he so-je-man[1] makee *l*ebel stand.

CHORUS.

Hang-cheong-low[2]—send 'um állo travellin',
Hi yah![3] Littee man can do!

   Dis Tai-ping
   He makee too much bobbe*l*y,
   Catchee man an' girley
   Makee kill-pidgin;
   Makee all he savvy[4]
   Of murder an' *l*obbe*l*y,[5]
An' cuttee off he pigtail to show he 'ligion.

---

[1] *So-je-man*, soldier or officer (C.V.)
[2] *Hang-cheong-low* (Cantonese), to take the long journey, *i.e.*, to be transported to the frontier.
[3] *Hi* or *ai yah!* an interjection, look!
[4] *Savvy*, knew.   [5] Robbery.

Jus' 'bout tim
Of állo dis 'citeyment,
Inside olo Joss-house[1]
'Way in Honán,
Burnin' plenty Joss-stick,[2]
To pay 'um[3] enlightyment,
Lib one good olo Joss-pidgin-man.

Dis Joss-man
Was a ve*ll*y good clirical,
Largee-facey man,
Belly ve*ll*y big,
By'mby he p*l*ay—
Makee first-chop mi*l*acle,
For he makee fat, jis' like he a ve*ll*y p*l*itty pig.

Pig keepee *g*lowin'
Fatte*l*er an' fatte*l*er,[4]
Nevva such a piggy
Since pigs began.
Joss-man he smilee,
An' talk, "You be flatte*l*er,"
When t'hey talkee pig look-see all-samee Joss-pidgin-man.[5]

---

[1] *Joss-house*, temple.
[2] *Joss-stick*, a kind of consecrated tapers made of sandal-wood.
[3] *Pay 'um*, to give them.
[4] Fatter and fatter.
[5] When they said the pig exactly resembled the priest.

THE REBEL PIG.

Long-side he Joss-house
Stop one olo manda*l*in,
He wantchee t'at pig,
He look-see 'um nightey day,
He talkee big lie
'Bout he f*l*in[1]—but állo slanderin',
Nevva can makee to catchee piggy 'way.

But one dark nightey
He sha-man[2] he got away
Wit' big sharp knifey
To ca*ll*y out he plan,
He crawley in he hog-pen,
An' t'here he cut away
He tailey of he piggy of he Joss-pidgin-man.

Nex' day Joss-man
Wailo talkee[3] manda*l*in
How la-li-loong[4]
Steal he piggy-tail.
Wantchee to catch 'um
One tim' a wande*l*in'[5]—
Pay 'um a floggin' an' sendee off to jail.

---

[1] *Flin*, friend.
[2] *Sha-man*, servant (unusual, but from a Chinese-English vocabulary).
[3] *Wailo talkee*, went and told.   [4] *La-li-loong*, a thief.
[5] Wandering.

"Hai yah!" say manda*l*in,
"Wat dis pidgin[1] now?
My muss do my duty
Juss as my can;
If piggy no hab pigtail
He catchee no 'ligion now,
An' my take 'um fo' one *l*ebel an' a Tai-ping man.

"T'at law talkee so-fashion:
Who catchee no piggy-tail
He makee 'bellion,
Muss die in de lan'."
My sing-song be finishee,
My hope you like my biggee tale
Of manda*l*in who cheatee he Joss-pidgin-man.

Tsow - une - shaw - wei.
(Hab finishee head and tail.)

NOTE.—The Tai-ping rebels cut off the pigtail, but suffered the hair to grow all over the head.

---

[1] *Pidgin*, affair.

The Green-Tea Land.

ONE PIECEE SING-SONG CALIFORNEE-SIDE.

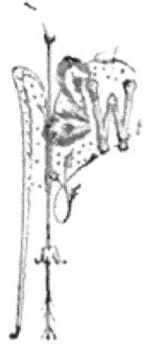

HAT-TIM he almon' flower hab white,
    when peach-t*l*ee blongey pink,
My smokee opium-pipe, galaw, an' muchee tim my tink
    'Bout állo pidgin China-side no fan-kwei understand,
In olo Fei-Chaw-Shang inside—my nicee G*l*een-Tea Land.

Some tim my makee d*l*eam-pidgin an' *l*idee on he wind
Ac*l*oss he *yaong* (he ocean) to állo my leavee 'hind,
Where willow-t*l*ee—all-same golo[1] in sun-go-down-shine stand,
In olo Fei-Chaw-Shang inside—my nicey G*l*een-Tea Land.

---

[1] *Golo*, gold.

My hearee one tim China-side flom velly olo witch,
Supposey my go fan-kwei¹ land, my gettee plenty lich.
What-tim my catchee pay dirt now, an' cash come plenty hand,
My wailo hom to Fei-Chaw-Shang—my olo Gleen-Tea Land.

T'here bottom-side he shiney moon at housee I look-see,
An' fishee 'mong he lô flower long-side he lunyan-tlee;
Supposey die, my catchee glave where wisee man command,
All plopa China-fashion in he nicey Gleen-Tea Land.

---

¹ Foreign devil.

My Heart and Gong.

MY paylo[1] all, my catch no more
   S'pose cumshaw p*l*opa be
   Inside[2] an' ghūnga állo store
My blong to paylo thee.
He ghūnga s'pose you *nik-ki*,[3] peal
   More largee any bell,
Long-side one piece inside t'hat feel
   Two-tim he ghūnga tell.

Suppose one-tim inside no good,
   Or no can do, maskee,[4]
T'hat ting he betta undastood
   What-tim you *ho-hop-ki*.[5]
Supposee ghūnga fally down
   An' makee catch a st*l*ain,
Oh, takee to one China-man,
   He makee p*l*opa 'gain.

The first eight lines of this rhyme are from an anonymous parody, which was written in ordinary English.

---

[1] *Paylo*, give.   [2] *Inside*, heart.
[3] *Nik-ki*, to hit or strike (unusual, C.V.)
[4] Anyhow.   [5] Drink tea (unusual, C.V.)

Proverbs.

WHO man swim best, t'hat man most gettee
    d*l*own;
  Who *l*idee best, he most catch tumble-
    down.

One piecee blind man hea*l*ee best, maskee;
One piecee deaf man makee best look-see.

One-tim in taushan wise man no talk *l*ight,
One-tim in taushan foolo shinee b*l*ight.

Supposey you no make look-see for mo*ll*ow,
You ve*ll*y soon to-day make catchee so*ll*ow.

One piecee farmer for t'hat *l*ain make p*l*ay,
T*l*aveller chin-chin for sunshine állo day.

You catch no needle sharp at both he ins,
You blongey no all-good man 'mong you f*l*ins.

Suppose you savvy wat t*l*ee day come by,
You catchee plenty dollar, f*l*in—*fa ts'ai!*

One man who never *l*eedee,
    Like one d*l*y inkstan' be;
You turn he top-side downy,
    No ink *l*un outside he.

You tongue he soft—you tongue he long tim last.
You teet'h he hard—but teet'h he wailo fast.

    Supposey you one top-side man,
        No squeezee man below;
    Suppose you blongey bottom-side,
        Let top-side be, galow.

You no hab pidgin, you no *l*ite or *l*eed;
One *l*oad no t*l*avel catchee plenty weed.

Suppose one man much bad—how bad he be,
One not'her bad man may be f*l*aid of he.

L'Oiseau.

NE-TIM two piecee Flunsee[1] walkee in Canton,
Look-see one piecee culio-shop—first-chop numpa one.

Chinaman he show 'um állo pukkha ting,
Birdee paint top-sidee plate—makee fly wit'h wing.

Flunsee look-see birdee—Flunsee talk "*Oiseau;*"
Chinaman he tinkee Flunsee ask "Why so?"

He no savvy Flunsee talk, so he makee tell
To 'um in he English—"*Why so?*—makee sell."

By'mby on lacker-box all-same birdee playin',
Flunsee-man look-see it, talk "*Oiseau*" again.

Chinaman he hear-lo—tink he savvy well,
So talkee all-same pidgin, "Why so?—*makee sell.*"

Flunsee tinkee sartin he hab larnee word,
Talk he flin t'hat *makisél* be China for a bird.

---

[1] *Flunsee* or *Flansy, i.e.,* Flançais, a Frenchman. Also *Fa-lan-sai* and *Fat-lan-se.*

The Princess in Tartary.

BELONGEY China Emp*e*lor,
    My make one piecee sing:
He catchee one cow-chilo,[1]
    She waifo Tartar king,
Hab lib in colo lan',[2]
    Hab stop where ice belong,
What-tim much so*ll*y[3] in-i-sy[4]
    She makee t'his sing-song:
"He wind he wailo[5] 'way,
    He wind he wailo 'long,
An' bleeze blow ove*l*y almon'-t*l*ee,
    An' ca*ll*y[6] a birdo song.

"Too muchee li[7] to China-side
    T'hat-place he t*l*ee g*l*ow high,
My fáta[8] blongey palacee,
    All golo[9] in-i-sy,

---

[1] Daughter (unusual).   [2] Cold country, *i.e.*, Tartary.
[3] In grief.
[4] *In-i-sy*, inside; not in common use, but given in this form in Chinese vocabulary. *In-sy* is, however, sometimes heard.
[5] Goes.   [6] Carry.   [7] *Li*, a Chinese mile.
[8] Father.   [9] Gold inside.

My wantchee look-see máta,[1]
He máta wantchee kai,[2]
My tinkey Mongol fashiono
No plopa[3] fashion my.
Ai! wind he wailo 'way,
Ai! wind he wailo long,
An' bleeze blow ovely almon'-tlee,
An' cally a birdo song!

"He birdo wailo Pay-chin,[4]
Chop-chop[5] he makee fly;
T'hat máta hear he sing-song,
How muchee dáta cly,
'How Tartar-side he colo,'
How muchee nicee warm,
One dáta-chilo catchee
In-i-sy[6] he máta arm.
Ai! wind he wailo 'way,
Ai! wind he wailo long,
An' bleeze blow ovely almon'-tlee,
An' cally a birdo song.

"He go top-sidee cow,
T'hat fashion Tartar-side,
T'hat no be plopa fashion
For Pili-kai[7] to lide.

---

[1] *Máta*, mother.   [2] *Kai*, daughter (unusual, C.V.)
[3] *Plopa*, proper.   [4] *Pay-chin*, Pekin.   [5] Quickly.
[6] Inside, within, in.   [7] Emperor's daughter.

Supposee he lib homo,[1]
    So-fashion he look-see,[2]
He *l*ide fo'[3] piecee horsey
    In coachey galantee.[4]
        Ai! wind he wailo 'way,
        Ai! wind he wailo long,
    An' bleeze blow ove*l*y almon'-t*l*ee,
        An' ca*ll*y he birdo song."

He máta talkee Pili :[5]
    He Pili open han',
He talkee, "No good fashion
    Hab got in Tartar lan'.
Must make one China town,
    Must makee for he kai ;[6]
Must makee Tartar-sidee,[7]
    An' he no makee c*l*y."
        Ai! wind he wailo 'way,
        Ai! wind he wailo long,
    An' bleeze blow ove*l*y almon'-t*l*ee,
        An' ca*ll*y he birdo song.

He sendee muchee coolie,
    He sendee smartee man,
He makee China city
    In-i-sy t'hat Tartar lan'.

---

[1] Home. [2] She would appear thus. [3] Four.
[4] Grand. [5] The mother addressed the Emperor.
[6] Daughter. [7] In Tartary.

He kai catch p*l*opa palace
 An' coachey galantee,[1]
No more hab makee c*l*y c*l*y.
 My sing-song finishee.
  Ai! wind he wailo 'way,
  Ai! wind he wailo long,
An' b*l*eeze blow ove*l*y almon'-t*l*ee,
 An' ca*ll*y he birdo song.

---

[1] And a fine coach.

The Rat.

Lou-shu-lai-kek-teng,—" A rat pulling out a nail."
Chinese Proverb.

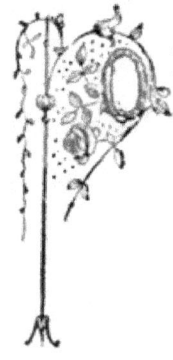NE-TIM one piecee *l*at
Pull hard to catchee nail,
And talkee when he come :
" Look-see what largey tail !

" But now my gettee out
T'his ting no good—no *how* [1]
One piecee olo iron
No blongey good chow-chow."

Supposey man lose tim
'Bout one long foolo tale,
He take you in—*P'ho !*
It all-same *l*at an' nail.

---

[1] *How*, good (M.)

The Pigeon.

"Pigeon-eyed man nestles in high places."
Chinese Proverb.

ONE piecee pidgin makee nest
    Top-side one Joss-house up to sky,
    One olo hen he wantchee know
    What for he pidgin lib so high?

He pidgin talk, "You savvy, f7in,
    My eye make ve7ly good look-see
Sometim to catchee chow-chow, or
    When hawk come t'his side catchee me."

Suppose one man belongey smart,
    He állo-way catchee pidgin-eye;
Who-man he makee good look-see,
    T'hat man he állo-way 7isee high.

Little Jack Horner.

PITTEE Jack Horner
   Makee sit inside corner,
      Chow-chow he C*l*ismas pie;
   He put inside t'um,
   Hab catchee one plum,
     "*Hai yah!* what one good chilo
        my!"

The Toyman's Song.

MILEY girley, losy boy,
  S'posey makee buy my toy;
Littee devilos make of clay,
Awful snakey clawley 'way,
Glate black spider, eyes all led,
Dlagons fit to scaree dead.
Dis de sortey plitty toy
Sell to littee China-boy.

NOTE.—My no can tinkee wat devilo Massa tinkee wat-tim he makee dis sing-song. It look-see my állo one piecee foolo-pidgin. Wat-for Chinaman makee littee devilos, snakey spiderlo an' dlagon, if no makee fo' chilos to scare 'um an' makee good? My tinkee can do good pidgin, supposey Englishee-man, insteadee pay he chilos one piecee plitty dolly, all-same one littee wifey, pay 'um littee devilos an' snakeys an' talkey, "S'posey you no belongey good, t'hat ting he catchee you all over, an' bitee you, galaw."

Supposey one piecee gentleum who leed dis, wantchee come dis pidgin in he family—my catchee one Chinee flin in London—he catch fai-dozen box first-chop China toy—makee sell too-muchee cheap, galaw. My too-much likee do littee pidgin long-he.

AH CHUNG.

Captain Jones.

ONE-TIM one piecee Englishman, he Jones
He *lowdah*,¹ gunboat captin blong he
　　pidgin
Makee big bobbery an' fight Chinee;
Maskee² t'hat China-junk he floggum much,
Pay 'um *fo-yok*³—t'hat talkee " gunpowda"—
An' makee English gunboat *ossoty*⁴
· Go bottom-sidee wata, állo fire.
What-tim he Captin Jones look-see he boat
Go walkee bottom-sidee so-fashion,
He talkee so one boy—one China-boy—
" Supposey *l*un in cabin, gettee my
T'hat piecee desk—*fitee* !⁵ or no can do !"
T'hat desk belongey inside muchee golo,⁶
Plenty chop-dolla', plenty piecee watch,
Plenty bank-note, *galaw*. He China-boy
Wailo⁷ chop-chop in cabin; by'mby-lo

---

¹ *Lowdah*, boat captain.　　　² *Maskee*, however.
³ *Fo-yok* (Cantonese), fire-physic, *i.e.*, gunpowder.
⁴ *Ossoty*, quick, make haste.　　⁵ *Fitee !* quickly.
⁶ That desk had much gold in it.　⁷ Went away.

He walkee back—állo top-side he clothes
He catchee plenty wata—he look-see
Too-muchee fliten—talkee, "No can do,
Hab got too-plenty wata all-inside
Top-side he cabin. No can catchee desk."
Wat-tim he China-boy he talkee t'hat,
One piecee largee cannon-ball—ch'hoy!
Come an' *cham-taw*—t'hat talkee Englishee,
"Cut off he head"—he blongey dead, galaw.

One piecee séli-man[1] he walk t'hat side,
He catchee all-same China-boy all-dead.
It blongey he pidgin[2] to takee boy
An' t'hlow 'um in he wata. Captin Jones
Talkee chop-chop to he, "You no can do,
You no ought makee so-fashion. You stop!
My wantchee look-see someting—my hab catch
Tinkee inside."[3] That Captin Jones look-see
That China-boy he pocket—*Ai! ph'ho!*[4]
He catchee inside állo dolla' t'here,
An' állo watch an' állo bankey-note
That blongey desk—all plopa pidgin he!

MORAL-PIDGIN.

That China-boy he plenty smart inside,
He plenty savvy. No piece English boy

---

[1] *Séli-man*, sailor (C.V.)   [2] It was his business.
[3] I have got an idea.   [4] Chinese interjections.

Can makee do all-same fashion, *galaw*,
Chop-chop like China-boy—he no can catch
T'hat dolla' all-same tim; he Captin Jones
He catchee smart inside—*he* tink chop-chop
T'hat boy hab catch he dolla'—that-fo'[1] he
Hab stop too muchee long tim China-side,
Suppose he no hab stop in China-side
He no t'hat much can savvy. China-boy
He catch t'hat dolla', an' t'hat Captin Jones
He catch 'um 'nother tim, an' állo two
Hab makee China-fashion. Sing-song done.

NOTE.—Dis ve*ll*y good sing-song, but my no tinkee Massa catchee p*l*opa fashion to talkee so wat t'hat China-boy wantchee do. My tinkee t'hat China-boy he savvy Captin Jones hab too much pidgin,[2] an' got too-muchee fightee to makee to take good káli[3] állo t'hat dolla'. So he take ca*l*'um[4] to give 'um to Captin Jones chilos o' f*l*ins, s'posey he get killee. S'posey you *tinkey* one piecee man stealee, you not ought talkee t'hat, an' takee way he facey. T'hat no p*l*opa China-fashion, t'hat no be p'lite.

AH CHUNG.

---

[1] *That-for*, because.   [2] Was too busy.
[3] *Káli*, care (C.V.)   [4] *Take cal'um*, take care of them.

The Ballad of Wing-King-Wo.

ALL-SAME one peachee flowero top-side he
　　gleen leaves walk,
　　Jist so one piecee sing-song go top-side
　　common talk.
　　An' man who makee sing-song top-side all
　　men, galow!
　　My sing you plopa stoly 'bout man name
　　Wing-King-Wo.

One Ing-he-lis Joss-pidgin-man stop China-side one-
　　tim,
He catch dis piecee China-boy an' take fo' wait on
　　him.
Hab catch 'um in he Wong-hau-kai—t'hat talk
　　Queen's Load, Hong-Kong—
He no can tink t'hat ting he make get plintee in a
　　song.

T'his China-boy he too-much wise, he numpa onelo
　　smart,
He hear-lo állo, look-see all, an' keep insidee heart.

S'pose Massa talkee *l*eason — he *l*oll¹ he eyes, *galow*,
An' make kow-tow an' tankee—t'his g*l*ateful Wing-King-Wo.

T'his Joss-man name he *L*o-pin-son, he wailo f*l*om Hong-Kong,
Hab walkee hom to Ink-i-lan—take China-boy along,
'Cause China-boy he talk he die s'pose Massa leave 'um so,
He wantchee die by Massa's side—t'his lovin' Wing-King-Wo.

He Massa' give 'um p*l*opa clo'se² an' muchee good advice,
He *l*oll he eyes an' hear-lo, an' say, "You talk so nice,
It makee my more good t'han clo'se—an' clo'se be nice, galow."
He makee numpa one chin-chin—t'his p*l*itee Wing-King-Wo.

He look all-same one gentleum asho' in Ink-i-lan;
He talk so nice, you nebba say he piecee sa'van³ man.

---

[1] *Roll*, *i.e.*, rolled up his eyes as if astonished.
[2] Clothes.   [3] Servant.

Wat-tim he walkee out to walk, he takee book,
  galow,
An' alloway hab spectacle—t'his larned Wing-King-
  Wo.

By'mby-lo people talkee he one poo' Manda*l*in
T'hat wantchee catchee savvy,¹ but no catch cash or
  f*l*in.
An' so all-same one sa'van come to Ink-i-lan, galow.
He ve*ll*y inte*l*estun man—dis touchin' Wing-King-
  Wo.

T'hey talkee him 'bout 'ligion—he muchee like to
  hear.
T'hey askee if he likeum, he talkee, "Nevva fear!"
T'hey tellum Chinee-fashion all came f*l*om debilo,
He *l*oll he eyes an' nod he head—t'his tender Wing-
  King-Wo.

By'mby-lo he leave Massa, wit' tear inside he eyes,
But to he p*l*opa station he savvy he must *l*ise.
Can-be you tink he take on airs wit' noblemen,
  oh no!—
He walkee 'bout wit' cla'gyman—t'his modes' Wing-
  King-Wo.

---

¹ *Savvy*, here learning, information.

T'hey talk, "We hear you Mandalin;" he smiley, shake he head,
An' say, "My no such g'lanti man—my no can buy my blead.
My only one poo' schola'—an' t'hat not much, you know—
T'hough I be first-chop in China," talk bashful Wing-King-Wo.

An' állo ting go nice fo' he one-tim in Ink-i-lan.
Some lady like to talkee t'hat handsome Chinaman,
So muchee girl make love-pidgin what-side he makee go,
He be one sassy flowa'-heart[1]—t'his pleasant Wing-King-Wo.

One nightey in a party he be top-side of all.
One piecee lady on he arm he plomenadee hall,
When állo once a gentleum cly out, "Hey debilo!
Wat-tim you comee flom Hong-Kong, my olo Wing-King-Wo?"

T'hat Wing-King-Wo he smiley an' talk, "My flin, I see
You takee my for not'ha man who face all-same as me."

---

[1] *Flower-heart*, a fickle lover.

He gentleum he talkee, "My no mistake, galow.
You wait on Massa *Lo*-pin-son, you name be Wing-King-Wo."

He Chinaman he look at 'um in ve*ll*y g*l*ate sup*l*ise,
An' puttee han' top-side he ha'at[1] an' softly *l*oll he eyes,
An' say, "You catch my name all *l*ight—but t'hen you shu'ly know
T'hat many taushan Chinaman he name be Wing-King-Wo."

One not'ha gentleum here come up an' say, "Sir, t'his Chinee
Hab pass examination—hab catchee big deg*l*ee."
He ot'ha say, "Supposey t*l*ue—my likee fo' you go
To look-see t'hat diploma of Massa Wing-King-Wo."

Now Wing-King-Wo hab tinkee t'his fo' many day befo'
It no belongey *l*eason to catch no chop to show,
So he take out he letta-case—all-same one cu*l*io—
An' open big diploma t'hat belongey Wing-King-Wo.

He gentleum he take 'um. As soon as he look-see
That big ve'milion paper—all p*l*intee in Chinee—
He tumble in one easy-chair an' laugh like debilo,
He sc*l*eam an' kick, he laugh so much an' c*l*y to Wing-King-Wo.

---
[1] Heart.

He talkee, "You no savvy, boy, how my can *l*eed Chinee.
Dis papa' he one sing-song-chop—one playbill, as I see;
It talkee 'bout a t'heata' in Hong-Kong a yeah' ago.
T'his be first-chop diploma for one man like Wing-King-Wo."

T'hey finishee to laughee—an' look—to much su'-p*l*ise,
T'hey no can find t'at Chinaman—he vanish f*l*om he eyes.
Hab muchee man in Lan-tun town—but f*l*om t'hat tim I know
Of no man t'hat look-see he face of Massa Wing-King-Wo.

MORAL-PIDGIN.

Supposey you poo' sa'van man—supposey you look-see
One chance to be one gentleum—all-same t'his poo' Chinee,
Can-be you no would make all-same—can-be you no begin,
But my would no make bet too-much upon it—O my f*l*in!

My tinkee t'hat one Chinaman all-same in heart as you,

But sometim *littee* smarta'—you savvy t'hat is t*l*ue.

Suppose one man he too-much poo' an' too-much smart, you know

He often come t'he pidgin on—all-same as Wing-King-Wo.

Note.—Dis állo one too-muchee pukkha sto*l*y. My savvy t'hat Wing-King-Wo, my tinkee he catchee one littee shop inside Sze-tan-lee-kai (dat talkee Stanley St*l*eet), inside Hong-Kong to-day. My no can ixcuse dat foolo Chinee all-same Massa do —my tinkee he catch one jackass-head, he too-muchee foolo to make 'pology fo'. Wat-fo' he wantchee talkee he all-same g*l*anti man China-side, when he savvy hab got too-muchee Ink-i-lis gentleum in Lan-tun who savvy him? Wat-fo' he wantchee make look-see pidgin how he one schola', when evely-body in Lan-tun jist as *l*eddy to *l*un afta' one piecee coolie, s'pose he got good clo'se? An' wat-fo'—s'pose he *must* makee look-see he schola', wat-fo' he no catchee one look-see-pidgin diploma, all-same as one Ink-i-lis man buy fo' fai dolla' f*l*om one piecee *l*ascal who make'um in Ame*l*ica? One piecee China-man wat no savvy nuf fo' dis must hab got wata top-side. My wishee Massa be mo' stric' wat-tim he *l*ite dis mo*l*al-pidgin. Hab got some Chinaman dat catch bad mo*l*als all-same fan-kwei, an' my no wantchee p*l*aise one Chinee, suppose he no good.   Ah Chung.

STORIES.

STORIES.

Captain Jones and the Arrow.

APTIN JONES nother-tim make fightee China-side, muchee big piece bobbe*l*y make he. Chinaman blongey war-junk he shootee too muchee a*ll*ow, Chinaman he holla', "*Hwan-na-kon!*" (t'hat talkee, "Fo*l*eign dog!") Captin Jones talkee, "Dam!" By'mby one piecee a*ll*ow come t'his side, he a*ll*ow stick in one China boy blongey Captin he boat. Captin he wailo chop-chop, he wantchee pullee a*ll*ow outside t'hat China boy; he pullee, pullee ve*ll*y muchee; no can do. Captin talkee, "My too muchee so*ll*y inside—no can makee so-fashion. He a*ll*ow no come outside. Maskee my talkee you what can do. My can put all-same one piecee Yin-ke-li[1] flag top-side he a*ll*ow—supposey you wave 'um. *T'hat* can do. *T'hat* nicey pidgin for you!"

---

[1] *Yin-ke-li*, English.

Captain Jones and his Medicine-Chest.

CAPTIN JONES, what-tim he catchee *ping-ch'wahn* (t'hat talkee, gunboat), belongey too plenty man catch sick. Captin hab one box állo full plenty *yow* (t'hat talkee, medcin); maskee he Captin no savvy what-for to payum. He makee come állo he man, he talkum, "Look-see. My hab got plenty, plenty medcin, my no savvy what-for to pay he. Maskee my savvy how muchee medcin one piecee man one-tim belongey chow-chow. My catchee one piecee chop[1] top-side állo piecee medcin—he chop talkee how muchee must chow-chow one-tim. S'posey you no f*l*aid you get spilum die-lo, my pay you állo you sickee man one piecee *yow*, galaw." He sick man talkee t'hat pidgin ve*ll*y hood, he állo chow-chow medcin, he állo blongy well by'mby an' walkee.

By'mby England-side when one piecee f*l*in askee, "How hab got t'is pidgin állo maskee?" Captin he talkee so-fashee, "Ai yah! My hab payum medcin, by'mby *man-man*[2] állo *yow* wailo—my no hab more, only one largey piecee *yahng-yow*" (t'hat talkee, *opium*

---

[1] *Chop*, inscription, prescription, or label.
[2] *Man-man*, slowly, gradually.

in Manda/in; Canton-side he talkee *apeen*), "long-side one piecee scissors. My finishee állo, so-fashion. Hab got only one piecee sick man left. My makee so-fashion: my payum opium to make he sleep, t'hen takee *che-endza*" (t'hat scissors) "an' poke he to wakeum up. *Man-man* állo man well, állo *yow* wailo."

He Captin Jones he one piecee ve*ll*y cu*l*io man inside he mouth. Fan-kwei állo too muchee cu*l*io. Chinaman savvy how to cureum; supposee one piecee man *poo-shoo-foo* (t'hat talkee, *sickee*) better állo *fan-kwei*. No hab got Iŏh-Uong-Chü-Su (he Medcin Joss) outside China-side.

The Obedient Servant.

NO belongey so good *kuhnpanty* or *mafoo* (t'hat talkee, servan' man) állo so plopa as China-side. Sometim maskee he *too* muchee good, *galaw*. One-tim one piecee mandalin hab come to he house, too muchee long tim in nightey, állo man inside he catchee shleep. Mandalin he makee one piecee bobbely—*ph'ho!*—he makee *muchee* bobbely—by'mby he make ear-hear t'hat one piecee *mafoo* walkee inside. He cly too much largey, "What for you no come? What for you you no let my room-inside?" He mafoo talkee by'mby, "No can do. No hab got stockin' on. No can go fore-side, Massa, supposee my no catch stockin'. Wait—my put 'em on!" He Massa say, "Taidza!" (t'hat talkee China-fashion, "*Foolo!*") "Come, maskee, wit'h no stockin'!" He makee stop nother-tim, mafoo no come. He Massa too muchee angly, he cly, "What for no come now? Chop-chop!" He mafoo talkee, "No can come chop-chop. How can do? My makee what Massa talkee my—my takee stockin' off!"

Allo tim olo custom China-side to makee what

Massa talkee you to makee. Supposee someting no be állo plopa—t'hat Massa *he* pidgin, galaw. T'his stoly he come outside one piecee olo China book—he chop " *Kuang-lin-hsaio* "—t'hat talkee, " Bload Folest of *Laugh*." No hab fan-kwei stoly so plopa as China stoly.

Howqua and the Pearls.

OLO Howqua, he one piecee ve*ll*y largey Hong má-chin, sartin before-tim you plenty hearee all-same Howqua. He catchee plenty dolla'. One-tim one piecee Me*l*ican gentleum talkee long-side Howqua, he talkee állo 'bout pearlee. Olo Howqua he talkee, "My wifee she ve*ll*y cu*l*io 'bout pearlee; she blongey so-fashion, she likee one kind pearlee, no other chop¹ can do. Supposey my catchee pearlee other fashion, galaw, she no look-see 'um." Me*l*ican he askee, "What fashion pearlee she likee?" Howqua talkee, "Belong so-fashion. Suppose t'hat pearlee numpa one *l*ound, he whitey colour look-see all p*l*opa, belong too much largey—állo-same inside palace that Empe*l*o' catchee topside he manda*l*in hat—suppose wantchee buy, pay t'hat golo-man plenty dolla'—supposey belong so-fashion, my wifey too muchee likee, galaw. What ting *you* tinkey?"

Supposey you hearee plenty talkee 'bout *fashion*. Ch'hoy! my tinkee China-woman, fan-kwei woman,

---

¹ *Chop,* kind or sort.

állo woman, állo tinkey állo-same inside he mouth. What ting you pay plenty dolla', he állo tim good fashion. Catchee plenty dolla', t'hen állo tim you catchee first-chop fashion. *Fa ts'ai!—fa ts'ai!*

The Cow and the Compradore.

ONE-TIM one mornin' belong tiffin-tim in Canton one piecee fan-kwei no catchee milk for chow-chow. He talkee comp*l*adore, "What for no got milk?" and makee one big bob-be*ll*y. Comp*l*adore he too muchee f*l*aid, galaw. He talkee gentleum, "My ve*ll*y much chin-chin you, you hearee my talkee. Supposey no can catchee milk, how fashion can do?" That *fan-kwei* talkee, "You no can makee so-fashion. Catchee milk belong your pidgin. You savvy you catchee one piecee cow makee milk, hab got one dog look-see he, one piecee woman take careum. What for no can do?" Comp*l*adore he too muchee f*l*iten, he c*l*y out one piecee sing-song—

> "T'hat cow hab die-lo,
> T'hat dog hab wailo,
> T'hat woman catchee chilo—
> How can catchee milk?"

Supposey sometim you go China-side, you hearee t'hat sing-song. Now my hab talkee you what for he makeum. And when one piecee man talkee you t'hat pidgin, supposey you say, " My *l*eedee t'hat long tim go in one piecee book—he first-chop pukkha book—s'posey you buy-lo." (Massa pay my cumshaw for talkee him állo t'his.)

The Chinese and the Jew.

ONE-TIM one Jew-man lib Californee-side makee one big piecee bobbe*l*y long-side one Chinaman. He cállo Chinaman plenty bad name; he cállo *la-li-loong*, all-same tief-man; he too muchee saucy, galaw. By'mby Chinaman no likee t'his pidgin, he ve*ll*y ang*l*y, he talkee Jew so-fashion, " *Ch'hoy!* You one big piecee foolo-man. Allo man talkee you foolo, you no chow-chow *chu-me-lung*, he nicey pigtail d*l*agon—what you cállo 'loin of pork.' My savvy you. You bad man—you ve*ll*y bad man—you too muchee bad.

" You too muchee bad, by Gosh!
You killee Me*l*ican-man's Josh."

Sometim my hear-lo Me*l*ican-man say, " By Josh!" My tinkee he stop China-side, he catchee t'hat word f*l*om Josh. Me*l*ican-man catchee plenty China word. Chinaman cállo he fast opium-boat *fa-hai-teng* (that talkee, *fast clab*); Me*l*ican-man he cállo one piecee fast horse "fast c/ab" all-same. Melican talkee "first-chop," and say he makee someting "so-fashion." Massa pay my one piecee cumshaw for talkee he t'his pidgin.

The Woolly Hen and the Red Goose.

ONE-TIM one piecee yunki sho-je-man[1] come China-side, t'at ting talkee one *gliffin*,[2] he no savvy too muchee, galaw. He f*l*in he sé-li-man what-tim he lib ship-side makee he big foolo, talkee he plenty big lie 'bout wat belongey China fashion.

One day t'his yunki sho-je-man catchee chow-chow long-side he f*l*in inside Canton. Yunki gentleum he talkee, "What for my no look-see állo tim my stop t'his side not one *woolly hin*, not one *hoong* (t'at talkey *l*ed) goose?" He f*l*in say-lo, "What foolo-pidgin t'at you talkee? How can hab woolly hin—how can hab *l*ed goosey?" He yunki man talkee, "My savee, maskee, plenty t'at ting belongey China-side. One piecee takta[3] ship-side talkee my t'at pidgin; my savvy t'at takta-man, he no talkee *sah-hwong*"—t'at one lie.

He f*l*in talkee, "My bettee you one han-tun[4] dolla' you no look-see one woolly hin, not one v'milion-color goosey, állo China-side." Yunki man he bet, he makee

---

[1] Young officer.   [2] *Griffin*, a new-comer.
[3] Doctor.   [4] Hundred.

come he shaman,[1] one China boy, he talkee him állo, askee t'at boy if he hab look-see woolly hin, *l*ed goose, China-side.

T'at China boy he catch much smart inside. He talkee, "Sartin hab t'at ting iniside, but he no be plenty, galaw. He woolly hin, he *l*ed goose he állo Joss-pidgin ting—Joss-man no wantchee fankwei to look-see t'at. No hab in Canton, állo t'at pidgin inside land. Maskee," he talkee, "suppose Massa pay my tunti, tatti[2] dolla', my wailo look-see pi[3] one piecee pukkha hin-goose for Massa."

T'at China boy he wailo look-see he Chinee f*l*in; my tinkee he hab muchee pidgin, galaw, állo t'at nightey. *Sún-sún*[4] mornin' he Massa hear-lo one ting outside, talkey, "*Cluk-luk-luk-lukky;*" nother piecee ting talkey, "*Wis-sis-sis-sis-sis.*" He gentleum talkee, "Wat dam ting hab got iniside? what for debilo makee állo dis bobbe*l*y?" He look-see outside—hab got one piecee woolly hin dat look-see állo same fashion one piecee littee two-leg sheep, galaw! Long-side hab got one piecee goosey, he goosey állo same color one fire-c*l*acker. Yunki gentleum he too muchee glad inside, he callee China boy, he talkee he "hood[5] boy" —he pay-lo one piecee cumshaw.[6] China boy talkee, "My stealee he hin-goosey inside one Joss-house. Must pay-lo back; supposey Joss-man savvy you catchee

---

[1] Servant. [2] Twenty, thirty. [3] *Pi*, buy.
[4] Very early. [5] Good. [6] Present.

t'at ting he killee you—sartin." Yunki man he go look-see he flin, he too muchee sassy, galaw. China boy walkee behind side he, he hab got hin-goose iniside he arm. Yunki man look-see flin, he shpeakee,[1] "Wat ting you talkee this-tim? Supposey you tinkey no hab woolly hin—supposey no hab led goosey—supposey my one piecce dam foolo, galaw? Ch'ho![2] wat you tinkey now?" He flin no savvy wat tinkey, állo must pay-lo he one han-tun dolla'. He look-see t'at állo plopa pidgin; hin hab got wool állo pukkha, goosey hab got plopa colour all-same. Empelor posha[3] he name top-side galantee chit.[4]

China boy no stop 'chee[5] tim, he talkee, he wantchee too much to wailo long-side hin-goosey to Joss-house, he káli[6] payum back to Joss-man. My tinkey t'at China boy catchee too muchee-muchee smart inside, my flaid supposey hin-goosey hab stop largey tim inside fan-kwei house he catchee sickee, galaw; he fedders by'mby belongey stlate all-same. nother hin, he goosey no led, állo he colour spoilum. T'at muchee pity, galaw, suppose he hin-goose catch sickee, so he hood China boy takeum wailo,[7] he so much hood heart iniside he no wantchee look-see t'at poo' goosey gettee white, all-same one sick man.

---

[1] Speak, say.
[2] An interjection.
[3] *Posha*, write (unusual, C.V.)
[4] Grand letter.
[5] Long, *i.e.*, muchee.
[6] *Káli*, want, care.
[7] Away, back.

The Talking Ducks.

NE piecee Chinee one-tim belongey Californee-side, he walkee, he look-see one piecee littee housee, t'hat place he Me*l*ican man dig golo.¹ Me*l*ican man chin-chin Chinaman supposey *sit-tsik*,² Chinee he makee állo maskee, he makee sit-tsik, he catchee hab-tim,³ he look-see two piecee duckey walkee top-side wata, he talkee chee-chee,⁴ "*Kwok-wok-wok, yok-ok-kok*." Chinee he make ear-hear állo duckey talkee, t'hat man catchee plenty muchee *l*eason China-side.

By'mby Me*l*ican askee what for he makee he sit still so muchey tim, what for he look-see duckey; Chinaman say, "My hear-lo, my savvy állo he duck talkee, my catchee t'hat pidgin China-side, galaw." Me*l*ican chin-chin⁵ t'hat Chinaman talkee wat ting he duckey hab talkee. Chinee hear-lo nother tim,⁶ by'mby he talkee, "Duckey talkee so-fashion—he shpeakee,⁷ 'To nightee must catchee too muchee

---

¹ Gold. ² Sit down (unusual, C. V.) ³ Leisure.
⁴ *Chee*, long, a long time. ⁵ Beg.
⁶ Again. ⁷ Says.

*l*ain, galaw, no blongey so muchee *l*ain t'his-side longa tim.'" Me*l*ican talkee, "S'posey t'hat állo maskee,¹ betta my savvy t'hat ting t'han catchee taushan² dolla'."

T'hat Chinaman stop t'hat-side állo nightey an' what he hab talkee t'hat állo p*l*opa pidgin an' come t*l*ue. T'hat nightey he hear-lo sún au-sai³ he *l*ain come chop-chop⁴ top-side house, plenty much. By'mby, b*l*ight-sun, what-tim Me*l*ican man look-see he, Me*l*ican talkee, "Supposey my no hab savvy what-tim he *l*ain come, t'hat all-same so bad my lost taushan dolla'." Maskee he no givee t'hat Chinaman cumshaw,⁵ not one littee nip-te-cashee,⁶ he too shmallo man inside, he no makee p*l*opa fashion, *p'ho!*

Chinaman sit down to-tim,⁷ he hearee duckey talkee, "*Kwok-wok-wok, yok-ok-ok.*" Me*l*ican he talkee, "Wat ting he duckey talkee t'his tim, galaw?" Chinee laughee, he say, "T'hat one piecee duckey talkee nother duckey; he say, 'Supposey you wantchee too muchee golo,⁸ no can do here. Must wailo ou-sy,⁹ what-side t'hat big t*l*ee belongey,¹⁰ t'hat-side catchee too plenty golo; supposey you dig that-side. T'hat állo p*l*opa.' Duckey savvy t'hat golo-pidgin, he állo-tim walkee t'his-side, t'hat-side look-see dirt. Suppose you makee

---

¹ Right, true.   ² One thousand.   ³ Early outside.
⁴ Quick.   ⁵ A present.   ⁶ One little small coin.
⁷ Sat again (two times).   ⁸ Gold.
⁹ Go outside, *i.e.*, **away (C.V.)**   ¹⁰ Is.

wat-ting¹ he duckey talkee, you makee p*l*opa pidgin-maskee."²

Chinee he wailo, Me*l*ican he tinkey t'hat ting állo maskee; he makee dig—makee muchee dig; he pay ou-sy plenty taushan dolla', all-same he no catchee golo. T'hat pidgin állo sickee.³ Muchee day muchee moon by'mby t'hat Chinaman ko-hom.⁴ T'hat-side, he look-see t'hat Me*l*ican, Me*l*ican makee iron-facey at Chinee. Chinee he make laughee inside he mouth,⁵ maskee⁶ he no make show, he no talkee, he look-see állo-same one piecee littee chilo. Chinee he talkee, "Hab catchee golo?" Me*l*ican talkee, "Dam you duckey!—no hab got golo." Chinee he sit downy nother tim all-same side, he duckey come, talkey, "*Kwok-wok-wok*"—all-same before-tim. Me*l*ican talkee, "Wat ting he duckey talkee t'his tim, my wantchee savvy?"⁷ Chinee he shpeakee,⁸ "He duckey talkee, Supposey one piecee Chinee tellee you wat ting állo-same one taushan dolla' hood for you,⁹ you no pay-lo¹⁰ he one cumshaw,¹¹ you muchee smart inside. Supposey nother tim t'hat Chinee pay you what duckey talkee, s'posee you tinkey *t'hat* állo maskee, you one piecee big foolo—you too muchee foolo, galaw."

One piecee Chinee-man, he my f*l*in, hab makee t'his

---

¹ That which.   ² That which is right.
³ That business languished.   ⁴ Returned.   ⁵ To himself.
⁶ However.   ⁷ Know.   ⁸ Said.
⁹ Anything worth to you a thousand dollars.   ¹⁰ Give.
¹¹ Present.

pidgin Californee-side—he talkee my állo t'his iniside Ning-po. My f/in talkee plenty /eason. He shpeakee, "Supposey you makee one piecee man muchee hood pidgin, supposey t'hat man too-muchee shmallo iniside to pay-lo you cumshaw—állo-tim t'hat man belongey foolo—sometim you easy makee cheat he. He állo-tim foolo." Massa no foolo, Massa all-tim pay my largey cumshaw for tell he China-fashion sto/y.

The Little Wife.

CHINAMAN he makee állo-tim[1] so-fashee[2] China-side. Supposey one piecee fáta[3] flog he bull-chilo,[4] supposey t'hat chilo too muchee largo man, all-same[5] olo man — he must catchee floggum, no other ting can do, wat-tim fáta nik-ki[6] he. Can makee c*l*y-c*l*y, no more can do. All-same fashion, put-lut-ta[7] floggee yang-shee-lut-ta,[8] yeung-ki floggee nip-pa,[9] ha-sze-man[10] floggee waifo,[11] máta[12] floggee kai-chilos,[13] massa floggee kung-pat-to,[14] kung-pat-to floggee sha-man.[15] Supposey one Chinaman hab catchee waifo—by'mby maskee[16] he gettee nother piecee waifo. He numpa one waifo talkee[17] "largo[18] waifo" China-fashion,

---

[1] Always.   [2] Thus in China.   [3] Father.
[4] Son.   [5] Be he a large or an old man.
[6] *Nik-ki*, strike (unusual).   [7] Elder brother.
[8] Younger brother.   [9] Nephew.   [10] Husband.
(All these terms for relatives are from a Chinese vocabulary, but are unusual.)
[11] Wife.   [12] Mother.
[13] *Kai-chilos*, *i.e.*, cow-children, daughters.
[14] Compradore.   [15] Servant.   [16] However.
[17] Is called.   [18] Large, here meaning superior.

numpa two he talkee "*likki* waifo."[1] Allo t'his pidgin belongey[2] olo cutsom. Supposey numpa one waifo floggee likki waifo, likki waifo no can do,[3] must catchee floggee all-same supposey[4] t'hat numpa one waifo belongey he máta. T'hat p*l*opa pidgin for he.

One-tim one Chinee má-chin[5] he blongey two piecee waifo. Numpa one waifo he ve*ll*y likki,[6] numpa two he one piecee ve*ll*y largo woman, all-same she catchee too muchee floggee, numpa one flog t'hat other waifo állo tim. Numpa two no can do one ting.

One nightey he má-chin he waifos hea*l*ee one piecee big bobb*el*y outside house. T'hat belongey one han-tun la-li-loong[7] wantchee catchee he one che-sze (chessy) full nip-ti cashee[8] hab got too-plenty dollar in-i-si.[9] Má-chin he too muchee f*l*iten, waifo numpa one she too muchee f*l*iten, állo makee c*l*y-c*l*y, galaw. Numpa two he littee waifo, she no káli[10] for la-li-loong[11]—what fashion you tinkey she makee? She catchee one piecee sword—she wailo bottom-side housee—she open *mun* (t'hat talkey *door*)—she talkee tief-man he *Nu-ts'ai!*[12] She talkee, "Who man you come t'his-side? My pay you floggum, *sheou-chu-shang!*[13]

---

[1] Little wife.   [2] Pertains to.   [3] Can do nothing.
[4] All just as if the head wife were her mother.
[5] Merchant.   [6] Small.   [7] One hundred robbers.
[8] A chestful of ready cash.   [9] Inside.   [10] Care.
[11] Thieves. [12] *Nu-ts'ai!* slave!   [13] You little beasts.

—*Sa-ni-ko-tow.*[1] He fightee hood, he cham-tow [2] one piecee la-li-loong—t'hat woman he no káli for la-li-loong. By'mby he tief állo wailo—numpa two t'hat shmallo waifo he wailo in-i-si house. She no *cly-cly,* t'hat-tim numpa one wifey too muchee *cly-cly.*

Plenty man come chop-chop, he állo wantchee savvy what fashion he likki waifo [3] hab larn fightee pidgin, how can do swordee. He numpa two talkee, "My fáta [4] he teachee sword, no hab man China-side savvy so good sword-pidgin [5] all-same my fáta. He tai-pai [6] swordman—he makee my larn t'hat ting before-tim.[7] Supposey you one piecee good swordman, you no káli [8] for one han-tun la-li-loong [9]—ch'hoy ! [10]—he no can do."

Allo man tálkee 'hood [11] to likki waifo, wat fashion he makee állo so p*l*opa, how galanti [12] fashion hab make t'hat numpa one waifo no catchee kill. Allo man chin-chin he, Pili [13] he hear-lo, he make pay-lo cumshaw.[14] Waifo numpa one he lose face,[15] he too muchee shame, he plenty so*ll*y inside [16] he so muchee hab nik-ki [17] he shmallo waifo. Not'har tim he no nik-ki he shmallo waifo, by'mby he likee [18] he too muchee, galaw, all-same kai.[19]

---

[1] I'll cut off your heads.   [2] Cut off the head.
[3] Second wife   [4] Father.   [5] Fencing.   [6] Chief.
[7] Long ago.   [8] Care.   [9] Robbers.
[10] Ha !   [11] Kind, good.   [12] Grandly.
[13] Prince, here the Emperor.   [14] Gave a present.
[15] Was much ashamed.   [16] Grieved.   [17] Struck.
[18] *Shee-hwan,* loved.   [19] Daughter.

Fire and River.

ONE-TIM plenty man fo*l*eign debilo go inside country, makee chow-chow. Englishman he talkee [1] *pic-nic* — China-side no got. By'mby állo man finishee chow-chow; plenty man too muchee d*l*unk. One piecee g*l*iffin [2] talkee he boy, "Just now my wantchee smokum pipe. Chop *na-ho lai!*"—belong Englishee talkee, "Pay my t'hat *l*iber!" T'hat boy wantchee laugh, he too muchee f*l*iten—thinkee he massa ve*ll*y d*l*unk, no savvy what ting he talkee. He massa look-see t'hat boy no makee wailo, tinkee he no hab hear, he ve*ll*y largey talkee he, "*Na-ho-lai!*" maskee t'hat boy no can sabby, talkee he massa, "No can do." He massa wantchee flog he; t'hat boy makee c*l*y-c*l*y, talkee, "How fashion my can pay *l*iber?" He master talkee he, "My no wantchee *l*iber—my wantchee *fire.*" And t'hen he massa talkee so-fashion, állo China boy makee laughum. "Blong massa talkee Chinee, no hab talkee p*l*opa. Massa talkee, '*Na-ho-lai!*'—pay

---

[1] Calls it.
[2] *Griffin*. A new-comer, a greenhorn (Anglo-Indian slang).

my t'hat *liber!* nother-tim massa more betta talkee,
' *Na-huo-lai!*'—blong pay my t'hat *fire!*"

Englishman no can talkee Chinee, he no plenty smart inside. Allo Chinaman talkee Englishee all plopa—all-same my.

Norval.

MY name blong Norval—top-side t'hat too
    high mountain
    My too muchee ólo fáta pay t'hat sheep
    he chow-chow.
    He smallee-heart man; too muchee take care
    catchee t'hat dollar, *galaw!*
    He wantchee my stop t'his side, countee my
    his own piecee chilo;
My no wantchee—my hab hear talkee t'hat fightee-
    pidgin,
My like fo' long t'hat Manda*l*in knockee állo man.
Littee tim Joss pay me what ting my fáta no likee
    do.
Last nightey t'hat moon get up *l*ound, állo-same my
    hat,
No get full-up, no get square;
Too muchee quiri (queeree) man come down t'hat
    hill;
Catchee t'hat sheepee, catchee long t'hat cow
He own take care him away.

My go catchee my f*l*in—my own eye hab see
What-side t'hat *l*obber-man walkee.
He no care him away—he pocket too muchee fill up,
Hi yah! my largee heart t'hat tim my hab go hom,
My no likee take care t'hat sheep long t'hat cow.

Anonymous.

Excelsior.

THAT nightey-tim begin chop-chop
   One young man walkey, no can stop,
   Maskee snow, maskee ice,
   He ca*ll*y flag with chop so nice
      Top-side galow !

He muchee so*ll*y—one piecee eye
Look-see sharp—so—all-same my,
He talkey largey—talkee st*l*ong,
Too muchee curio—all-same gong.
      Top-side galow !

Inside house he can see light,
And eve*l*y *l*oom got fire all *l*ight,
He lookee plenty ice more high,
Insidee mouth he plenty c*l*y,
      Top-side galow !

Olo man talkee, "No can walk,
By'mby *l*ain come—ve*ll*y dark,
Hab got water, ve*ll*y wide."
Maskee, my must go top-side,
    Top-side galow!

"Man-man," one girley talkee he,
"What for you go top-side look-see?".
And one tim more he plenty c*l*y,
But állo-tim walkee plenty high,
    Top-side galow!

"Take care t'hat spoilum t*l*ee, young man,
Take care t'hat ice. He want man-man."
T'hat coolie chin-chin he, "Good-night!"
He talkee my can go all *l*ight,
    Top-side galow!

Joss-pidgin-man he soon begin
Morning-tim t'hat Joss chin-chin,
He no man see him plenty fear,
Cos some man talkee he can hear
    Top-side galow!

T'hat young man die, one large dog see
Too muchee bobbe*l*y findee he.
He hand blong colo—all-same ice,
Hab got he flag with chop so nice,
    Top-side galow.

MORAL.

You too muchee laugh ! what for sing
I tink so you no savvy t'hat ting !
Supposey you no blong clever inside,
More betta *you* go walk top-side,
      Top-side galow !

This anonymous parody of "Excelsior" was introduced to the reading public in "Macmillan's Magazine" and Mr Simson's entertaining work "Meeting the Sun."

[In concluding these Ballads and Stories, the author has only to add that he would be greatly obliged to those of his readers who would kindly send to him (care of N. Trübner, Ludgate Hill, London) any specimens of Pidgin-English, whether in prose or rhyme, letters, anecdotes, sayings, &c., and especially any words or phrases which do not occur in the following vocabulary.]

PIDGIN-ENGLISH VOCABULARY.

PIDGIN-ENGLISH VOCABULARY.

IN this Vocabulary *C. V.* indicates that the word is taken from a Chinese vocabulary of Pidgin-English, *M.* that it is Mandarin-Chinese, and *Canton*, from the Canton dialect. These Chinese words are seldom or never heard in pure Pidgin, but their utility in certain cases is manifest. For the Mandarin words I am indebted to "Chinese Without a Teacher," by H. A. Giles; for those from the Chinese Vocabulary, to a MS. version by Prof. R. K. Douglas; and for many other terms, as well as for much kind assistance and suggestion, not only to these gentlemen, but also to Ng Choy, Esq., of Lincoln's Inn, to Mr Th. A. Arnett, and Mr R. Scott Walker. I have in this collection also given many Anglo-Indian and other words not strictly Pidgin, but as they are constantly occurring in it, or are used by Englishmen and Americans in China, they have a certain relation to the dialect.

A.

Ah-kwan-tsae, gentleman.
Ai! Hai! a very common interjection. It frequently precedes *yah*.
   Hai yah! fan-kwei lo! Ha, foreign devils! (foreigners.)
Allo, áll-o, all; every.   "Allo man talkee my so-fashion."
All-plopa, quite right.
All-same, like; as; similar; identical; agreeing with.
Amah, a Chinese nurse. Hindu, *ayah*. In Mandarin dialect, *lowmar*.

Au-lo—*i.e.*, olo, old. (C.V.)
Au-sai, outside. (C.V.)

B.

Bad heart, used to express all forms of evil-mindedness. "You belongey too muchee bad heart."
Banjee (Anglo-Indian?), band of music.
Barbly, babble; noise. *Too muchee barbly*, too much noise.
Before-tim, formerly; once; previous; previously.
Belongey, Blongy, Blong, indicates the pertaining to in a very wide sense. Also applied to quality. "You belongey too muchee saucy, galaw." "My belongy Consoo boy"—I am the Consul's servant. "You belong clever inside"—You are intelligent. "You belongy foolo."
Bobbery (pron. *bobbely*), the English slang word, but extended in Pidgin-English to signify every kind of noise, disorder, quarrel, disagreement, fuss, and trouble. "This my flin, he wantchee makee one littee piecee pidgin long-side you. S'posey you cheatum, my makee big bobbely wit' you."—*Newspaper*. Vide *Barbly*.
Boilum, to boil. "My boilum tea."
Bottom-side, below; down; under; low.
Bright-sun, to-morrow—*i.e.*, *ming-yat*. (Canton; not in use.)
Bull-chilo, male child. Becoming obsolete.
Bund, quay; embankment. (Hindu.)
Bunder, a report; canard; a story which has obtained currency on the quay or *bund*.
By'mby, by-and-by, or any future time or occasion; after; afterwards; again.

C

Cab-tun, captain.
Callee, curry.
Candareen, a coin (seldom seen), value one penny. In Chinese, *Fan*.
Can do, indicates, like "yes?" many forms of ability or possibility—*e.g.*, Can you? Is it possible? It is possible. A mandarin seeing a small English sailor thrash a large one, exclaimed, "*Hai yah!* littee man *can do*." "My no can do that" may mean "I *will not* do it."
Cango (Japanese), a kind of couch or litter, carried under a pole by two men.—*The Eastern Seas, by Capt. B. W. Bax.*

Cangue, a frame used to confine prisoners; a kind of movable stocks, through which the head is passed.

Cash, the only current coin in China, value one-tenth of a penny. In Chinese, *Li*.

'Casion, occasion; reason; cause. "You no 'casion makee so-fashion."

Catchee, to get; have; own; possess; hold. "My look-see one piecee man catchee chow-chow"—I saw a man eating. "My catchee waifo"—I am—or am to be—married. "My no catchee one f*l*in inside allo that housee"—I have not one friend in all that family.

Catty. "The unit of weight for metals used in Asia, equal in China to 600·399 grammes; in Siam, 613·468."—*Larousse.* "A Chinese weight equal to 1 lb. 4 oz. It is also used in Japan, Batavia, and other parts of India. A weight of 3 grains used in the East for weighing precious stones."—*Richardson.*

Char, chair; a sedan-chair.

Chee, long. Probably an abbreviation of *muchee*. (C.V.)

Chee, or **Jee**, the common termination for words ending in *t* or *d*—*e.g.*, *want*, want*chee*.

Che-sze—*i.e.*, **Chessy**, chest; box. (C.V.)

Ch'hoy, a meaningless, but common and very expressive, interjection.

Chilo, child.

Chin-chin, to worship (by bowing and striking the chin); to reverence; adore; implore; to deprecate anger; to wish one something; invite; ask.

Chinee, Chinese; Chinaman.

Chit, a letter. (Hindu.)

Chop, inscription; label; stamp; device; motto; ticket; characteristic. *Numpa one first-chop*, best; superfine.

Chop-chop, quick; quickly; fast.

Chow-chow, food; to eat. Specially applied to a kind of sweetmeat made of a great variety of material, *e.g.*, melon rind, bamboo sprouts, small fruits, &c. In India a variety of objects, or odds and ends in a basket, &c., is called *chow-chow*.

Chow-chow, to have a meal. In Mandarin, *chih fahn*.

Chu-me-lung, pig-tail dragon—*i.e.*, a loin of pork. Not used in Pidgin-English.

Chu-shung (correctly, **Sheon-chu-shang**), "you little beast," or animal.

Coco, a Japanese measure of rice.

Colo, cold.

Come-this-side, arrived here. "Just now hab 'got two piecee joss-house-man come-this-side"—Two missionaries have arrived.

Compradore, steward. In Mandarin, *mi-pahn*.

Consoo, consul.

Coolie, common man; labourer.

Cot-houso, court-house.

Cow-chilo, girl. Becoming obsolete.

Cow-oil, or **Cow-grease,** butter. Obsolete, but literally translated from the Chinese word for butter.

Culio—*i.e.*, curio, curiosity; queer; odd; strange; peculiar. *Curio-shop*, curiosity-shop.

Cumshaw, a present.

Cutsom—*i.e.*, custom, applied to law and habits, &c. "T'hat blongey olo cutsom."

D.

Deen-seen-hong, the Eastern Extension Australia and China Telegraph Company, Shanghai.

Devilo, or **Debilo,** devil.

Die-lo, die; died.

Dlinkee, to drink.

Dollar. Money or wealth is generally expressed by dollar. "He no hab catchee dollar"—He made no money.

Dragon, a favourite Chinese emblem and simile.

E.

Ee, a common termination put at will after almost any noun or verb. Walkee, talkee, fishee, dog-gee.

Ee-sheung, clothes. (M.)

E-ta-lee-kwoh, Italian. *E-ta-lee-kwok-kung-kwan*, the Italian Consulate.

F.

Facey, Facie, Facee, face; character; self-possession. *Loosee facey*, to loose character; to be put to shame; to be disconcerted.

Fai, five. (C.V.)
Fai, or **Fy**, a fire.
Fai-tee, quickly! be quick! "A pure Chinese phrase, but commonly used by Europeans." *Fitee-fitee!* very quick! hurry!
Fa-ke, American—*i.e.*, flower-flag. *Fa-ke-ling-se-koon*, the United States Consulate. (Hong-Kong.)
Fa-ke-kwok, flower-flag-nation.
Fa-lan-sai, French. Also *Flan-sai*, *Flun-see*, and in the "Directory," *Fat-lan-se*; in the "Amoy Directory," *Wo-lan-sai*.
Fan-kwei, foreign devil—*i.e.*, a foreigner.
Fan-yun, foreign man; foreigner.
Fasson, fashionable.
Fast crabs, smugglers. *Fa-hai-teng*. In America this term, or fancy, is applied to very fast-trotting horses.

"De fellers mit de vancy crabs
Pooled up to see him pass."—*Hans Breitmann*.

Fa ts'ai! fa ts'ai! get rich! get rich! A common courteous greeting. (M.)
Fei-chaw-shang, the green-tea country. (Canton.)
Feng-shuey, the Earth Dragon, (?) a spirit supposed to travel in the air; the geomantic influences of the earth, influencing lucky or unlucky places; luck or fate; elemental and occult influences.
Finishee, the common word for completed, done, finished, or accomplished.
First-chop, best; first.
Fi-sze—*i.e.*, Fishee, fish. (C.V.)
Flin, friend.
Flower-flag-man, American.
Flower-heart—*i.e.*, many hearts; fickle; wavering; generally said of lovers.
Fo, four. (C.V.)
Foo-lin—*i.e.*, Flin, friend. (C.V.)
Foolo, fool; full. (C.V.)
Foong-shun, "The Sailors' Home." (Shanghai.)
For-what? or, What for? why?
Fo-tin, fourteen. (C.V.)
Fowlo, fowl.
Fo-yok, fire physic. (Canton.)
Fung, male. (M.)

Fung-hwang, phœnix; a fabulous bird; the token of prosperity and happy omen; majesty; grace; colour. *Fung* is the male, and *hwang* the female phœnix. (M.)

G.

Galanti, grand; great. (C.V.)
Galaw, Galow, Galā, **Gola, G'low,** a word without meaning, used as an interjection, like *halt* in South German.
Girley, girl.
Glound (*i.e.,* ground or earth) **chit,** a telegram.
Go, used to indicate the future tense. "You go make that ting?" —Do you mean to do that?
Go-down, warehouse; small house, &c.
Golo, gold; golo-man, jeweller.
Good-talkee, Velly good-talkee, an excellent opinion or expression; eloquence.
Good wind! Good water! the Pidgin-English farewell to a friend starting on a journey.
Got—*e.g., Hab-got,* there is; *you got!* have you?
Grass-wood-man. "The Chinese call simple, rustic people Grass-wood-men."—*Celestial Empire,* July 24, 1875.
Griffin (Anglo-Indian), one newly arrived; a greenhorn.

H.

Hab, have.
Hab-got, is; there is; has.
Hăk-cha, black tea. (Canton.) *Hay Ch'ah* (M.)
Ha-loy, come down. (Canton.)
Handsome talkee, fine, agreeable, or ornate language.
Han-tun, a hundred. (C.V.)
Ha-sze-man—*i.e.,* Has-a-man, husband. (C.V.)
Have got wata top-side, mad; cracked; foolish.
Haw, to drink. (C.)
He, used for he, she, it, or they; often includes *is.*
He-foo, rise-fire—*i.e.,* a rocket. (Canton.)
Hing-ki-chi (C.V.), **Han-ker-choo,** handkerchief.
Ho,[2] river. (M.)
Hoan-lam, the Pencil forest—*i.e.,* the highest degree of literary graduates. (Canton.)

Ho-hop-ki, to drink (*unusual*). (C.V.)
Ho-lan-kwoh (*kwok*), Dutch.
Ho-ming, Reuter's Telegram Company is so termed in the "Shanghai Directory."
Hong, Hahng, a warehouse; applied specially to the great firms which formerly regulated all Chinese commerce. (M.)
Hoong, red. (C.)
Hop, have. (C.V.)
Hop, half. (C.V.)
Hop-fa-sze—*i.e.*, Hab fasson, fashionable (*not much used*). (C.V.)
Hop pi-tsin—*i.e.*, Hab pidgin, have business.
Hop-tai—*i.e.*, Hab die, dead. (C.V.)
Hop-tim, leisure. (C.V.)
Houso, house.
How, good. (M.)
How-fashion, what for? why? what is the meaning? "How fashion you stop out so late?"
How-tak-tsei, very good. (M.)
Huo,[3] fire. (M.) *Na-huo³-lai,* bring fire.
Hwan, fire. (C.)
Hwan-na-kou, foreign dog. (M.)

I.

Im-koy, not ought. (Canton.) "Used politely accepting or asking for a civility; thank you."
Ing-ki (Inkee), ink. (C.V.)
Ink-e-li, English. *Ying kwo* (M.)
Inside, within; in; interior; heart; mind; soul; in the country. "You belongy smart inside"—You are intelligent. A Chinese, on being shown the picture of a locomotive, at once remarked, "Hab got too much plenty all-same inside"—*i.e.*, We have many such in the interior of China. "Hab got one piecee man, one piecee girley room inside." "Room inside," within.
Inside he heart, same as "Inside he mouth."
Inside he mouth, secretly in his mind; to himself; reserved.
In-sy, inside. (C.V.)
Iron-face—*teet-meen* (Canton); *t'eeay layeen* (M.)—stern; obdurate; cruel; severe.

J.

Jade, a hard greenish, green, or reddish stone, found in Tartary, much used for ornaments. Mandarin, *yŭ*.
Jah, to fry. (M.)
Jahn-fahng, a go-down; warehouse, &c. (M.)
Jahng-moo, a bill. (M.)
Jih-zee-pah-nee-ah, Spain.
Jin-rick-sha, a vehicle like a Bath chair, drawn by a man. (Japanese.)
Jin-rick-sha-man, a man who draws the jin-rick-sha.—*Celestial Empire*, Oct. 14, 1875.
Josh—*i.e.*, Joss, god; idol.
Joss, god; idol, &c. (From the Portuguese *Dios*.)
Joss-house, temple; church.
Joss-house-man, clergyman.
Joss-pidgin, religion.
Joss-pidgin-man, a bonze; priest; clergyman.

K.

Kai, daughter (*unusual*). (C.V.)
Ka-lan-ti—*i.e.*, Galanti for grand, great. (C.V.)
Káli, to want; care (*unusual*). (C.V.)
Ká-lin, to call. (C.V.)
Kam-kwat (called by Europeans *cum-kwat*), a kind of small orange. (M.)
Kam-ma-she-yun, commercial.—*Hong-Kong Directory*, 1875.
Kam-pat-to, compradore. (C.V.)
Kana-man, artillerist. (C.V.)
Kaou-lo, cold—*i.e.*, Colo in the common dialect. (C.V.)
Kilin—*i.e.*, Kleen, or Gleen, green.
Ko-au-sei—*i.e.*, go outside; return. (C.V.)
Ko-hom, return. (C.V.)
Ko-lock, clock.
Kong, a water-vat. "He fell into a huge water-kong."—*Celestial Empire*, Oct. 2, 1875.
Kow-tow, to incline before; bow.
Kuk-man, cook. (C.V.)
Kum-leen, golden water-lilies—*i.e.*, the small feet of Chinese women.

Kung-he! kung-he! congratulatory phrase on the birth of a child, or on success in examinations. (C.)
Kung-kwan, consulate.
Kwai, tortoise. (M.)
Kwei, a devil; devils.

L.

L, used by all Chinese for *R* in Pidgin-English.
Lahnt'o, lazy. (M.)
La-li-loong, a thief; thieves. "The barber complained he had been called a *la-li-loong*, the Pidgin-English for thief."—*Celestial Empire,* 1876.
Lan-tun, London.
Largee, Largey, Largo (*g* soft), much; great; magnanimous; loud. "My largo man, my have catchee peace, my have catchee war."—*Points and Pickings of Information About China* (London, 1844).
Larn-pidgin, an apprentice; a boy admitted by favour of the upper servants to a house that he may learn English and domestic duties. *Vide* Introduction.
Lau-tai, a ladder. *Lau-tai-kai,* Ladder Street.—*Hong-Kong Directory.*
Lay, thunder. (M.)
Layang yeendza, a tael. (M.)
Layeen, face. (M.)
Lee-pi, a week. (M.)
Leet'o, inside. (M.)
Li, a Chinese mile (pron. *lee*). "Although at the present day 250 *li* make a degree, they have varied in the past under different dynasties and in different provinces."—*Deguignes, Les Navigations des Chinois, &c., Mémoires de l'Académie, &c.* "He told as many *li*'s as there are between Canton and Pekin."—*Nine Stories of China.*
Li, to come. (M.) *Woa li la,* I have come.
Likki, little (*unusual*). (C.V.)
Lim, eleven. (C.V.)
Lin, rain—*i.e., l*ain. (C.V.)
Littee, little.
Liu-shu, willow. (M.)
Lo, a termination which frequently follows vowels or liquids—*e.g., die-lo,* die; *olo,* old.

Lod-yay, old father; **a term of respect.** (Canton.)
Lo-kwat, a fruit. (Canton.)
Long-side, with; by; near; accompanying.
Look-see, look; behold; appear like; see; appreciate; understand.
Look-see pidgin, ostentation; hypocrisy; sham.
Loosee, to lose. *Loosee facee*—*i.e.*, face, **to be dishonoured or shamed**; to lose reputation.
Love-pidgin, love; courtship; wooing; tenderness.
Love-love-pidgin, sensuality; voluptuousness. Applied to *erotica* in books or art.
Lowdah, captain of a junk, or servant in charge of a house-boat.
Lü, donkey. (M.)
Lü, green. (M.)
Lungan, the wild lychee-tree. (M.)
Lun-tun, London. *Lun-tun-ch'ün-kau-ui*, "The London Missionary Society" (in Staunton Street, Hong-Kong).
Lussu, stork or crane. (C.)
Lüt, red—*i.e.*, *l*ed. (C.V.)
Lychee, a fruit.

M.

Mace, a coin (seldom seen), value about eightpence. In Chinese, *Tsien*.
Ma-chin, merchant. (C.V.)
Mafoo, horse-boy; groom. "Talkee mafoo to come chop-chop!"
Mah, a horse. (M.)
Mah-tung, a stirrup. '(M.)
Mai-pan, compradore. (Canton.)
Makee, to make; do; effect; cause—*e.g.*, "Suppose you makee buy." It is almost generally prefixed to verbs to make them active.
Ma-kwa, a riding-coat.
Mandalin or **Mandarin,** a high state official or grandee. From the Portuguese.
Man-man, slowly.
Maskee, all right; correct; never mind; notwithstanding; nevertheless; however; but; anyhow. This word is used in a very irregular manner. It is not Chinese, its equivalent in Mandarin being *poo-yow-cheen*.
Massa, the common word for master.

Ma-sze-ki—*i.e.*, Mashkee or Maskee, it is all good. This form of spelling and definition, as given in the Chinese "Vocabulary of Words in Use among the Red-Haired People," indicates the original pronunciation and meaning of this perplexing word.
Máta, mother. (C.V.)
Maw, ink. (M.)
Mei-le-keen-kwok, American. (Canton.)
Melican, American.
Mi, to sell. (M.)
Ming-pak, bright-white—*i.e.*, to understand clearly. (Canton.)
Ming-pi, clever. (M.)
Ming-yat, bright-sun—*i.e.*, to-morrow. (Canton.)
Missee, miss.
Mississee, mistress.
Mit-chi-man, an officer's boy—*i.e.*, midshipman. (C.V.)
Molo-man (*i.e.*, *Moro*, a Moor), a negro.
Moon-pidgin, monthly.
More-betta—*i.e.*, better. "My more-betta go 'way"—Superior.
Mowdza, hat. (M.)
Muchee, very; intensified as muchee-muchee.
Mun-lee, money (*unusual*). (C.V.)
My, my; I; me; mine. Sometimes *we*, *our*, or *ours*.

N.

Na, no. (C.V.)
Nah, to take. (M.)
Nah-li, bring. (M.)
Na-hop—*i.e.*, No-hab, given as meaning *without* in the C.V.
Nai, nine. (C.V.)
Nai-foo, knife. (C.V.)
Nai-ti, night. (C.V.)
Nar? where? (M.)
Naw, you (*unusual*). (C.V.)
Nee, you; plural, **Nee-mun**. (M.)
Nep-fa-lan, Netherlands.
Nightey, night.
Nik-ki, to strike (*unusual*). (C.V.)
Nip-pa, nephew. (C.V.)
Nip-te kashe, "liberty cash"—*i.e.*, ready money (*unusual*). (C.V.)

I

Nītchky, a grotesque little image; a Japanese button for the girdle.

No-belong leason (*i.e.*, reason), it is not reasonable.

No-can, it is not good; I cannot; it will not do; impossible.

No can do, cannot. No can do? can you not?

No fear! in very common use in Pidgin-English.

Nother, another; other.

Nother-tim, again.

Not ought, should not. "You not ought makee so fashion."

Numpa one, number one; first-class; very. "Dat tea belongey numpa one"—*i.e.*, best. A Chinese servant being asked if a certain person lived in the house, replied, "Hab got top-side t'hat numpa one ugly Englishee lawyer, all-same so-fashion," accompanying the description with a significant grimace.

Nū-ts'ai, slave. (M.)

Nü-yen, woman. (M.)

O.

Olo, old.

Olo cutsom, indicates everything established or usual. "That belong olo cutsom."

One piecee, one piece; one; a; an. *One pe-sze* (C.V.) "You catchee one piecee wifey?"—Are you to be married, or, Have you a wife? In Canton, *yi-kozhen*.

One-tim, once; only.

Osso! Ossoty! be quick! make haste!

Outside, foreign. *Ngoi-kwok* (Canton), outside nation. *Wi-kwo* (M.)

Outside old river, the Yang-tse-kiang. *Ngoi-kong-lo* (Canton).

Outside-the-river-man, a man from the north of China. *Ngoi-kong-yun* (Canton).

Owmoon, Macao.

P.

P'ahndza, plate. (M.)

Pahngdza, maize. (M.)

Pak-tǎw-kwei, white-headed devils—*i.e.*, turbaned Mohammetans or Parsees. (Canton.)

Paou-cheong, or **Paou-tseong,** gunpowder; crackers. (Canton.)

Pā-pā-man—*i.e.*, barber-man. (C.V.)
Par-sa-mum, a tree bearing a luscious fruit.
Pa-ti-li, a priest. (C.V.) From the Portuguese *padre*.
Pay, to give; bring; deliver; transfer; as well as pay. *My pay he*, I gave him.
Pay-ching, Pekin. (M.)
Pay-wine, beer. (Canton.) *Pay-tsaw* (Canton.)
Pecul. "In commerce, an Indian measure, equal to 100 catties [vide *Catty*], or 132 lbs. avoirdupois."—*Richardson*.
Pee, pen. (M.)
Peedza, nose. (M.)
Ph'ho! an interjection.
Pi, to buy (*unusual*). (C.V.) "*Pi wat-ting*, to buy things."—*C.V.*
Pidgin, business; affair; occupation; a word of very general application—*e.g.*, *joss-pidgin*, religion; *chow-chow-pidgin*, eating or cookery. Probably the Chinese pronunciation of the word business (*Pi-tsin*, C.V.), according to others of the Portuguese *ocupação*.
Pidgin-English, English as imperfectly spoken by Chinese.
Piecee, Piecy, with the prefix one, signifies *a* or *an*, as well as piece or portion.
Pi-li, emperor (*unusual*). (C.V.)
Pi-me, raw rice. (M.)
P'ingdza, bottle. (M.)
Ping-ling, a girdle. (C.V.)
Pi t'ahng, sugar. (M.)
Play-pidgin, sham; humbug.
Plenty, much; very; very much. "He makee walkee plenty high."—*Parody of Excelsior*.
Plopa, proper; commonly used for good, right, correct, well, or nice, in the most extended forms. "Dat allo plopa pidgin"—That is all right.
Pomelo, a fruit.
Poo-poo, purple.
Posha, to write (*unusual*). (C.V.)
Powfoo, bundle. (M.)
Pukkha, true; real; genuine; best quality; the real thing.
Punkah, a machine for fanning.
Puttee, book. (Indian.) A term used on the completion of a contract. In a retail shop the term used for concluding a purchase is "*makee shuttee*." This Hindu term is used in contradistinction to *lutcha*, meaning imitative, unreal.

Q.

Quiri (query, qu?), curious; queer. From the parody of *Norval*.

R.
(*Vide L.*)

Room-inside, within. Pron. *loom-inside*.
Russki, Russian. Pron. *lusski*.

S.

Sa-ki, spirit made from rice. (Japanese.)
Sam, seven. (C.V.)
Same, generally used with *all*, *all-same*, which see.
Sam-pan, a Chinese boat.
Sam-shoo, rice spirits.
Sa-ni-kow-tow, I'll cut off your head. Often heard among common people. (M.)
Sassee, Sassy, saucy; proud. "You belongey too-muchee sassee, galaw."
Sa-van, servant.
Savvy, know; understand. *No savvy?* do you not know? (Portuguese.) Used in the widest sense.
Sé-li-man, sailor. (C.V.)
Sélum, sell. (C.V.)
Setty, Settee, settled; arranged; used in business when a bargain is agreed upon. "My have setty—can puttee book."
Se-wei-tun, Sweden.
Sha-man, servant. (C.V.)
Sha-pi (sabby, savvy), understand (*unusual*). (C.V.)
Shawt'o, tongue. (M.)
Shee, to wash. (M.)
Sheeang-kwah, melon. (M.)
Sheen, letter. (M.)
Shin, a good spirit. (Canton.)
Shleep, sleep. *Shi-lip* (C.V.)
Shmallo, small; mean; small-minded. *Sze-ma-lo* (C.V.)
Sho, hand. (M.)
Sho-cheen, towel. (M.)
Sho-che-man—*i.e.*, *sho-je* (or *sojer*) *man*—soldier. (C.V.)
Shoo, tree. (M.)

Shooey, water. (M.)
Showdza, spoon. (M.)
Shpeakee, to speak. *Sze-pik-ki* (C.V.)
Shummo, what; why. (M.) "*Nee way shummo poo li?*—Why don't you come?"—*Chinese Without a Master.*
Shu-sun-koon, General Post Office. (Hong-Kong.)
Sick, out of order; out of repair.
Side, place; country; situation. "What side you blongey?"—Where is your home? "He blongey China-side now"—He is in China. *Side* qualifies prepositions and adverbs—*e.g.*, *top-side,* above, or high; *bottom-side, far-side,* beyond; *this-side,* here; *allo-side,* around.
Sik-kan-mit, second mate. (C.V.)
Sik-sze (six-ee), six. (C.V.)
Sing-song, any dramatic or musical entertainment; a song; ballad; poem.
Sing-song-houso, a theatre.
Sit-tsik (shit-tsik), sit down (*unusual*). (C.V.)
Smellum-wata (water), eau-de-Cologne; perfume. "Pay my that smellum-water!"
Spi-lum, Spoilum, injure; to injure; rotten; decayed; broken. Very extensive in its applications.
Squeeze, a fine or imposition.
Sún, early; soon. (C.V.)
Supposey, suppose; if; admit. A word of very general application.
Sycee, silver; dollars bearing merchants' stamps.

> "Some ask me what the cause may be
> That Chinese silver's called sycee?
> But probably they call it so
> Because they *sigh* to *see* it go."

T.

Tael, a coin (seldom seen) worth six shillings and sixpence. (*Vide* "The Current Gold and Silver Coins of all Countries," by Charles Trübner.) In Chinese, *Siang.* "The Chinese terms for coins, except the *cash* or *li,* are, properly speaking, denominations of weight. The cash are coins cast of base metal, with a square hole in the centre. The media of payment in larger transactions are gold and silver ingots of variable

weights and fineness, and the Spanish and American dollars."
—*C. Trübner.*

Taidza (Tai-toze), idiot!

Tai-fo-neen, great examination year for **degrees**.

Tai-pai, a large ticket; a great chop.

Tai-pan, great series—*i.e.*, the first of a series—a head man; a "boss."

Tai-pay, great beer—*i.e.*, porter. (Canton.)

Tai-yun, great man; excellency.

Ták-ta, doctor. (C.V.)

Talkee, tell; say or talk; inform; ask. "He talkee my no can do"—He told me it was impossible.

Talkee-leason—*i.e.*, talk reason, moral or literary discourse; wise maxims or extracts.

Ta-mei-kwoh-tsung-ling-sze-yamun, the United States (American) Consulate General.

Tanka, egg-house—*i.e.*, a boat in which people live.

Tan-kwoh, Danish.

T'atti, thirty. (C.V.)

T'attin, thirteen. (C.V.)

Tau-shan, thousand. (C.V.)

Tau-ti, civil governor.

Ta-ying-ling-shi-shu, the British Consulate.

Ta-ying-sho-sun-kwan, the British Post Office.

Té, day (*unusual*). (C.V.)

Te-le (Tlee), three. (C.V.)

Té-li-man, tailor. (C.V.)

That, often used as indicating in Pidgin-English, when it would be omitted in ordinary English—*e.g., that man,* he.

T'hat, a peculiar and common pronunciation of *that*.

That-same, that.

That-side, there.

That-tim, then; when.

This-side, here. "Hab makee stop t'his side."

Tiffin, lunch. (Indian.)

Tim (Teem), time; is employed with all adverbs of time.

Tin, ten. (C.V.)

Tin, thin—*i.e.*, light, not heavy. (C.V.)

Ting, thing.

Ting-ki, thank you (*unusual*). (C.V.)

Tinkee, think.

Tin-mak, Denmark.

Toi-tche, German—*i.e.*, Deutsch.
To-lo-li, good; passable (tolerably?).
Too, very. "You too bad."
Too-muchee, very; excessive. "You too-muchee hansom"—You are very handsome.
Top-side, above; on high. "Top-side galow."—*Excelsior*.
Top-side piecee Heaven pidgin-man. Mr Francis, editor of the Troy *Times* (U.S.A), writes that a native convert designated the Methodist Bishop Harris by this epithet.
Tui-lip, twelve. (C.V.)
Tun-ti, twenty. (C.V.)
Two-tim, twice; again.

U.

Uli, shopkeeper (*unusual*). (C.V.)
U-lup, Europe.
Understand? a very common expression for Do you understand?
Ut (pron. *oot*—i.e., 'ood, 'hood), good (*unusual*). (C.V.) "Ut man"—Good man.

V.

Van-ts'ang-koon-sz, the Pacific Mail Steamship Company. (Shanghai.)

W.

Wai-fo (Wifey), wife. (C.V.)
Wai-li-ūt, good condition—*i.e.*, gone good (*unusual*). (C.V.)
Wailo, Wy-lo, go away; away with you! go; depart; gone; departed; went.
Walkee, to go, in any way. "China-man wear two watch. What for? Supposee one makee sick, t' other walkee."
Wantchee, to want.
Wat, what. *Wat fa-sze* (C.V.), what fashion; what kind. "What fashion you do that?"
Wata, water. "Hab got wata top-side"—Mad, foolish, cracked.
Wat-ting? what is it? what?
Wei-yuen, great officials.
What for? why? wherefore? because. "What for you makee so fashion?"

What-side, where. "What-side my can go?"—Where can I go?
What-tim, when.
White-ant, a female marriage-broker.
White-mice, Chinese babes of the poorer class. When blind, they are called *blind-mice*.
Who-man? who? "Who-man makee b*l*ake t'hat one-piecee glass?"
Willow-waist, expressive of a fine female figure.
Woa, I. (M.)
Woamun, we; us. (M.)
Woamunty, our; ours. (M.)
Woaty, my; mine. (M.)
Wun, one. (C.V.)
Wun pi-sze, one-piecee. (C.V.)

Y.

Ya-mun, Ya-men, a mandarin or prefect's residence; a consulate.
Yang-shi-butta, younger brother (*unusual*). (C.V.)
Yat, eight. (C.V.)
Yat-i-man, German. *Yat-yee-man-ling-se-koon,* the Austrian-Hungarian Consulate. (Hong-Kong.)
Yen,[1] swallow. (M.)
Yen[2] (*second tone*), goose. (M.)
Yeung-ki—*i.e.,* Unkey, uncle (*unusual*). (C.V.)
Ying-jen, Englishman. (M.)
Ying-ling, England. *Ta-ying-ling-shi-shu,* the British Consulate. (Shanghai.)
Ying-kwo, English nation.
Yin-ke-li, English.
Yu-loh, a shop (?); shopkeeper. (C.V.)

PIDGIN-ENGLISH NAMES.

The following Chinese renderings of personal or local names are taken from the Chronicle and Directory for China, Japan, and the Philippines for 1874 (Hong-Kong, "Daily Press" office).

Ae-mih, Eames.
Ah-li-feh, Oliver.
Akala, Agra, the Agra bank.
A-lee-pat, Albert.
A-lee-pat-tau, Albert Road (Hong-Kong).
Ap-pa-teen, Aberdeen.
A-pun-nee, Albany.
A-put-not-tau, Arbuthnot.
A-sze-ka-E-sze-mo, Hadji Ali Asgar H. Esmail.
A-tam-se, Adams.
Ba-la-tah, Brandt.
Be-da-be-se, B. Davis.
Bee-oz-bee, Bigsby.
Be-le-u, Bellevue.
But, Bird.
Chak-man, Chapman.
Chan-shi-lee-hong, Chancery Lane (Hong-Kong).
Cha-ta, Chater.
Cha-teen, Jardine (Matheson & Co.)
Cha-wai, Jervois.
Chim-me-son, Jameson (& Barton).
Dah-loong, Deslandes.
E-lee-kan, Elgin.
Em-pi-as-chow-tim, Empire Tavern.
Eoo-she, Vaucher.
E-pa-la-him, Ebrahim.
Fo-go, Vogel.
Fok-kun-na, Falconer.
Ga-lock-i-san, Gerlach (Dr).
Gip, Gibb.
Go-bu, Gottburg.
Got-te-le-yin-tsze-koon, Gutierrez, R. F., printer.
Ham-po-tsow-tim, Hamburg Tavern.
Hap-bi-boy, Habibbhoy.
Hee-lee-kai, Hillier Street (Hong-Kong.)
Ho-ching, Hutchings.
Ho-hwa-way, Rodewald.
Ho-la-da-wei-se, Holloday, Wise, & Co.

Ho-lee-ut, Hollywood.
Hom-see, Holmes (G.)
Hot, Heard.
How-wat, Howard.
Im-pai-pa-lew-wa-lee, Empire Brewery.
Ka-ham, Graham.
Ka-lo-lin, Caroline.
Ka-lut, Garrett (Miss).
Kao-lin (also Ko-lun-shi), Collins.
Kaou-yih, Cowie.
Kap-pi-lee-kai, Cleverly Street (Hong-Kong).
Kau-hung, Corne.
Kee-cheong, Russell & Co.
Kee-lee-mun, Gilman.
Kee-lee-sz, Giles.
Keng-ming, Cumming.
Kit-chi, Gage.
Ko-fu-kai, Gough Street (Hong-Kong).
Kok-lun, Cochrane.
Ko-lo-sa, Kruse.
Ko-lo-wit-se, Carlowitz & Co.
Koo-ka, Cook.
Kum-boo, Campbell.
Lai-tun-shan-tau, Leighton Hill Road (Hong-Kong).
La-man, Lamont.
Lam-mat-A-kin-shan, Lambert, Atkinson, & Co.
Lane-ka-la-fat, Lane, Crawford, & Co.
Lan-se-teen, Landstie
La-see-lee, Russell.
Lau-len-sie, Laurence.
Le-be-son, Robinson.
Lee-ma-ter, Lemaitre.
Lee-mee-ta-sz, Remedios.
Lee-nee, Rennie.
Li-na-oze, Reynolds.

Lo-cha-lio, Rozario.
Lo-ling, Rawling.
Lo-long-ya-yun-tze-koon, Noronha & Sons, Government printers.
Lon-tun-in, London Inn.
Lo-peen-sun, Robinson.
Lut-ta, Rutter.
Ma-ke-le-ga, Macgregor.
Mak-ken-chi, Mackenzie.
Ma-ko-wan, Macgowan.
Mak-ton-na, Macdonald.
Mak-tung-see, Maertens.
Ma-sha, Mercer.
Mat-chee-see, Melchers & Co.
Mat-ti-shan-ki, Matheson Street (Hong-Kong).
May-po-koh, Myburgh.
Mei-cha, Major.
Mo-lee-see, Morris.
Mo-le-se-hen-lee, Morris & Henry.
Mo-tee-kung-se, Moody & Co.
Mun-ham-tau, Bonham Road (Hong-Kong).
Mur-le, Murray.
Nee-boon, Kneebon (G. A.)
O-le-fun, Olyphant.
O-le-yan-ta-yeuk-fong, Oriental Dispensary.
Olo-bak, Overbeck.
Olo-pi-lee, Old Bailey.
O-ren-to-bar-an-bow-ling-al-ly, Oriental Bar and Bowling Alley.
Pak-ka-koong-se, Parker & Co.
Pak-tun, Purdon & Co.
Pa-lee, Birley.
Palo-kai, Burrows Street (Hong-Kong).
Pa-lo-se, Burrows.
Pa-lot-pi, Broadbear.

Pa-see-wai, Percival.
Pee-lee, Peil.
Pek-lik-het, Blackhead.
P'ih-hsiau-pooh, Bishop.
Pik-ka, Baker.
Pi-lee-kai, Peel Street (Hong-Kong).
Pin-ning-tun-kai, Pennington Street (Hong-Kong).
Pit-lit-che-sze-kai, Bridges Street (Hong-Kong).
Po-ling, Baldwin.
Po-long-ti-chong-sz, Brown, barrister-at-law.
Po-soo, Bourjau.
Pot-teen-cha, Pottinger.
Po-tung, Barton.
Qoong-deh, Thorndike.
Sai-mo, Seymour.
San-ta, Sander.
See-mit, Schmidt.
Seem-shun, Siemssen & Co.
Se-tak-ho-te-li, Stag Hotel.
Shae-lee-kai, Shelley Street (Hong-Kong).
Shap, Sharp.
Shap-tor-la, Sharp (Edmund) & Toller.
She-la-se, Schellhaas & Co.
Sing-fut-lan-sz, St Francis.
Si-sang-e-tsung, Johnston.
Sit, Sites.
So-may-foo-e-süng, Somerville, J. R., Dr (Foochow).
So-sha-yan-tze-koon, DeSouza & Co., printers.

Sow-ta-lan, Sutherland.
Sui-son-koon, Sailors' Home.
Sun-too-sz, Santas.
Sze-kat, Scott.
Sze-tan-lee-kai, Stanley Street (Hong-Kong).
Sze-ti-wa-li, Stavely.
Sze-to-i, Stewart.
Sz-tek-fun, Stephens
Tae-le, Telge,
Tak-ka-le-se, Douglas.
Tak-kee-la, D'Aguilar.
Tam-son-han, Thompson & Hind.
Tan-na, Turner.
Too-te-lee, Dudley.
To-por-so, Dubois.
To-se, Dods.
Tun-wo, Dunn.
Wai-le-ma, Wilmer.
Wai-ling-tun, Wellington (Hong-Kong).
Wai-lum, William.
Wak-ka, Walker.
Wak-lee, Wardley.
Wan-ham, Wyndham.
Wa-tai-lee, Water Lane (Hong-Kong).
Wat-sun, Watson.
Wat-te-kai, Witty Street.
Wo-uhl-sz, Walsh.
Yae-fan, Evans.
Yat-i-man-hak-tim, German Tavern.
Yen-kee, Jenke.
Yu-wai, Juvet.

By the same Author.

FU-SANG; or, The Discovery of America by Chinese Buddhist Priests in the Fifth Century. By CHARLES G. LELAND. Crown 8vo, pp. 232, cloth. 7s. 6d.

This work, which has been very extensively reviewed in England and on the Continent, will shortly appear in French.

THE MUSIC LESSON OF CONFUCIUS, and other Poems. By CHARLES G. LELAND. Fcap. 8vo, pp. viii. and 168, cloth. 1871. 3s. 6d.

An early reviewer of this book spoke of the author as gifted with melodious expression. This opinion has been confirmed by the fact that every song in "Confucius" has since been set to music, by Miss Virginia Gabriel, Carlo Pinsutti, and other composers, while several of the longer poems, e.g., the "Music Lesson," have found a place in such works as Whittier's "Three Centuries of Song."

THE BREITMANN BALLADS. The only Authorised and Complete Edition. In One Vol., including Nineteen Ballads illustrating his Travels in Europe (never before printed), with Comments by Fritz Schwackenhammer. By CHARLES G. LELAND. Crown 8vo, handsomely bound in cloth, pp. xxviii. and 292. 6s.

This edition contains more than twice as many ballads as any other, including the *whole* poem of "Breitmann as a Politician," and it has been thoroughly revised and annotated by the author. Within a year of their first appearance these Ballads were published in America, Canada, Australia, and two versions in England. In London "Hans Breitmann" appeared simultaneously on the boards of three theatres. There were innumerable imitations, poems, pamphlets, &c.; a newspaper was published bearing his name; there was even a brand of Hans Breitmann cigars. In fact, since this work was published, many of its phrases are proverbial wherever the English language is spoken, while Hans Breitmann has become generally recognised as a jesting nickname for Germany.—*Publisher*.

GAUDEAMUS. Humorous Poems translated from the German of Joseph Victor Scheffel and others. By CHARLES G. LELAND. 16mo, pp. 176, cloth. 1872. 3s. 6d.

Of this translation the "Augsburger Allgemeine Zeitung" remarked that if a club of half-a-dozen scholars were each to take it, without knowing the original, translate it into German, and then to reduce their work into a single perfectly edited text, the result would be Scheffel's own poems.

"The faithfulness and force of his renderings are alike remarkable."
—*Daily News.*
"These poems give in the translation, as in the original, infinite pleasure."
—*Magazin für die Literatur des Auslands.*
"A volume which shows merit of a very high order."—*Echo.*
"They are clever spirited bacchanalian lyrics, full of wild rollicking fun."
—*Saturday Review.*

THE EGYPTIAN SKETCH-BOOK. By CHARLES G. LELAND. Crown 8vo, pp. viii. and 316, cloth. 1873. 7s. 6d.

"The level of high animal spirits and perfect good-humour maintained throughout the volume—whether in the description of persons, of places, of incidents, or of customs and ceremonies—is as remarkable as it is refreshing ; and while the author gives a thoroughly realistic glance, or series of glances into the aspect and state of Egypt as it is in the present day, he keeps us in a state of chronic amusement, frequently broadening into downright ticklishness, and not unfrequently into uncontrollable laughter. Everything he touches on seems to suggest to him some piece of natural unstrained wit, and he never becomes prosy for a moment."—*Civil Service Review.*

"It is certainly one of the best books of the kind."—*Literary World.*

THE ENGLISH GIPSIES AND THEIR LANGUAGE. By CHARLES G. LELAND. Crown 8vo, cloth, pp. 276. 7s. 6d.

"This book deserves to be read with attention and with thanks. Mr Leland's pictures of the strolling Bohemians of our highways and byways are picturesquely drawn and coloured to the life. He has evidently about him that intuitive tact, or that magic of *bonhommie* which is needed to penetrate the freemasonry of this peculiar race and to draw out their esoteric lore."—*Saturday Review.*

"The only book since Borrow which gives us anything at once new and reliable concerning the fast-dying-out Bohemians of our native land. We can very heartily recommend it as readable as well as instructive."—*Standard.*

"A perfectly serious book of very great and pleasant interest."—*Hour.*

"Mr Leland has gone up and down among the people of whom he writes, and studied their goings-out and comings-in and all their ways. In entering into a familiar knowledge of the common life, and observing those little inner traits which constitute the characteristic, he has been very successful."—*Literary World.*

"Mr Leland must have bestowed years of study and research upon his subject to make his work so complete in every respect as it is."—*Observer.*

"This work, which was very extensively and favourably reviewed in England and Germany, contains fifty very curious and entertaining *Gudli*, or short stories, in Rommany and English, with collection of proverbs, and other gipsy folk-lore."—*Publisher.*

ENGLISH GIPSY SONGS IN ROMMANY, with Metrical English Translations. By CHARLES G. LELAND, Professor E. H. PALMER, and JANET TUCKEY. Crown 8vo, cloth. 1875. 7s. 6d.

"The authors of the 'English Gipsy Songs' have gone a step beyond any who have preceded them, in catching the picturesque and quaint characteristics of gipsy life, and clothing them in a metrical form."—*Saturday Review.*

"A very quaint and interesting volume, combining sound knowledge with literary skill, and **the result is** a work which may be recommended **as well to** the scholar as to **the ordinary** subscriber to Mudie."—*Athenæum.*

"We are delighted to **recognise** in the utterance of the muse of this gipsy Musagetes and his choir the clearness, the freshness, the sanity, the tender human feeling and simple fidelity to nature of that rare product in these times—true popular poetry. We could hardly name a modern **poetess, unless it** be Alice Carey, with a more decided bent for the concrete **and substantial, or** less addicted to her sisters' besetting sin of diffuseness **of phrase and dilution** of thought, than Miss Tuckey. A second 'Auld Robin Gray' from her pen would hardly surprise us."—*Examiner.*

"**Admirably complete** as well as interesting."—*Civil Service Review.*

"**An admirable and** tasteful volume."—*Nonconformist.*

MEISTER KARL'S SKETCH-BOOK. By CHARLES G. LELAND. New and elegant edition on toned paper, gilt edges and cover beveled. Crown 8vo, pp. 287, cloth. 12s. 6d.

Of this work, **which** has been most extensively and favourably reviewed, **the** late WASHINGTON IRVING wrote: "I trust it has met with a wide circulation, for such it merits by its raciness, its quaint erudition, its graphic delineations, its veins of genuine poetry, and true Rabelaisian humour. To me it is a choice book to have at hand for a relishing **morsel** occasionally, like a Stilton cheese, **or** *pâté de foie gras.*"

HEINRICH HEINE'S PICTURES OF TRAVEL. Translated by CHARLES G. LELAND. Crown 8vo, pp. 471, cloth. 7s. 6d.

This translation of the "Reisebilder," which appeared in 1855 and which is now in its *tenth thousand*, has attained the position of a classic of its kind, having been **most extensively, and in all cases favourably reviewed by the** highest literary authorities. An English edition, thoroughly revised by the author, **is now in course of preparation.**

HEINE'S BOOK OF SONGS. Translated by CHARLES G. LELAND. Very neatly bound, beveled, with gilt edge, pp. 239, cloth. 7s. 6d.

In this latest edition of a work which met with the same universal **critical** approbation as the translation of the "Pictures of Travel," every **poem is** in the same measure as the original, **while** the first line of each is **given in** German.

LONDON: TRÜBNER & CO., LUDGATE HILL.

www.ingramcontent.com/pod-product-compliance
Lightning Source LLC
Chambersburg PA
CBHW031501160426
43195CB00010BB/1057